Commoditized

How it Happened – and How You Survive

Commodotized

How It Happened – and How You Survive

by

Wade Burt

First Edition: [October 2014]
Printed in the United States of America
ISBN: [978-0-9886386-2-4]

To My Family,
To My Friends,

To those who don't yet know.

Table of Contents

Prologue

This book will expose to American citizens the changes in the workplace and labor market occurring between the late 1980s and well into the year 2014. We will discuss the collective impact of the events as we describe the different influencers on the American workforce and how they have combined to fundamentally change how America defines work, careers and success.

These discussions will include the influence of finance, government, labor, education and more in modifying the components that made the United States the country to which much of the world looked for hope and for the example of labor in a successful free market economy.

Certainly, as you read you will realize that keeping a career in a position to allow you to support yourself and your family in the United States is becoming a more challenging proposal. In addition, if you have children or grandchildren, their ability to support themselves and their families could be significantly more challenging.

In the process of writing, I discovered many situations that, when considered individually, do not appear to be very bad, but when considered together take on a much more sinister appearance, causing some of the book to feel a bit conspiratorial. Collectively, I believe there can be no doubt that the common interests of all

United States citizens, while they may appear to be in conflict, have been used to disassemble the American Dream. I am anxious to hear from those of you who have strong views on the subject. I am hopeful this book might be a wakeup call for the working class of the United States, if there even is such a thing. I am concerned that the working class is being replaced by a servant class.

I am not convinced that we are a divided country by anything other than by class. Surely, we have some racists, some classists, some elitists and many who do not treat others as they should.

Overall the working class has more in common than they have differences. With that in mind, I believe the history of dividing the working class is evident in the social engineering used to differentiate and sub-divide people in an effort to distract them from the real problems they face. Certainly, the progressives in both political parties have used social engineering to divide us, even separate us, in order to ensure we never find a reason to collaborate one with another. That social engineering has produced the commoditization of the American workforce, much to the detriment of the entire nation – even the world.

HOW THIS BOOK GOT STARTED

The book got its start around 2010 as I began to realize that I was going to have to change my approach to my career. As a healthcare IT consultant I had spent most of the previous ten years going from one job to another as I applied my skill implementing technologies in healthcare facilities.

In mid 2012, I made a decision that solidified the idea that the

American labor force – and I personally – had been commoditized. I had been blessed to be offered a full time position with a very large national company for which I had been consulting on a number of projects. As the Manager of Physician Technology, I had a comfortable six figure salary, a wonderful boss, an amazing team, a good office, great opportunities for growth both short term and long term, and the knowledge my career was finally set - at age 54.

I received a call from a large national recruiting firm, offering a position providing services to a number of their clients. They offered competitive benefits and salary. The opportunity would allow me to work from home. It had the prestige of a national engagement with a need for the specialized consulting I provided. They came at me full force – offering me all the things I already had, but telling me I could get more. Was this greed on my part? Probably – but I succumbed to their "wining and dining" and took the offer.

I resigned my fulltime position with one of the largest hospital companies in the United States to accept a position with one of the largest consulting companies in the United States. My first assignment was with another large hospital company, but it was not the same. I felt as if I had been deceived and felt a little humiliated. I was still a consultant, but I was being bought – and sold – by a company whose primary commodity was people.

A BETTER UNDERSTANDING

It began to be clear that the change was very fundamental. Many in our country had simply lost the ability to see what their role was in the workplace. As I studied those changes, I realized we had all become commodities - using our labor as "free agents" to support our families.

A few years prior, I had watched as some of the physicians I worked with entered a new and different arrangement with a healthcare provider. Rather than being in private practice, the model had them engaged as employees – and offered heavy performance measurement and incentives. I had considered then that the physicians were being commoditized.

As I discussed this relatively new condition with friends who have also joined the ranks of the commoditized, I realized that many of us had no idea how to be a commodity. In fact, most individuals have no idea they have been commoditized.

I also realized that many people had no idea of the changes that were necessary in order to be successful in the commoditized labor market. In our discussions, the talk often turned to a conversation of how we got to this point - how commoditization became the normal mode for the working class in the United States.

Many people are still building their careers for a market that had been conditioned to the days when a person's career path consisted of getting a job, maturing in that position, then working long enough to "retire". After that (if they were lucky), there was a home that had been paid for and a stipend of some sort (retirement?) that allowed them to no longer be required to go to work. By age 65 their lives were radically changed as they often had "nothing" to do in their retirement.

THE AMERICAN WORKER

I like to look at what causes people, particularly people in the American culture, to behave the way they do when they make decisions about their lives, families and careers. I also have become interested in what makes the government engage in social experiments to lead the population in a particular direction. Consider two of the different components of our society – the "middle class" and the "working class". These two very separate classes are sometimes treated as one. In fact, in history these two classes were often intermingled. I propose in the commoditized world that may not be the case.

I am personally grateful for the inspiration that comes to each of us to help find success in the trying times we face. I do believe we are each inspired to help one another - often in ways we neither expect nor understand. An idealist approach, to be sure, I know our careers can be so much more if we become engaged in giving others the benefit of our experience and knowledge. We don't really know or understand who needs to hear what we each have to say about our experiences, but mentorship can be a very rewarding experience.

I believe in the United States, we have to ponder the larger questions posed in a "free" society. What motivates the citizens to be fully engaged in their daily lives? What are the obligations, if any, of being citizens of a free Republic? Do we understand them enough to be active participants? What did this have to do with how the market has turned out to be so commoditized?

On a personal level, how do we make the choices that allow us to be happy? What is our motivation to make the choices we make each day? Is the motivator family, work, money, or something else? If money is the motivator, how do we decide what we will and will not do for it?

If the motivator is money, is it possible to have "enough"? And what happens when we finally do have "enough"? A bishop once told me "You can always make more money - but you can NEVER make more time".

One of my motivations for writing this book is the hope I can somehow help people decide when enough is enough and what brings them true happiness before they run out of the time of which they can never make more.

HOW TO STAY ALIVE

Finally, the book came about as a result of the need I observed in many people for methods that will enable them to survive in the workplace market as they go about raising and supporting their families. One thing is certain; the life of a commoditized worker will be very different from that of what was at one time a much more regimented labor market.

I am afraid that some of the content of this book reads like a group of conspiracy theories. That was not a deliberate effort to spell out that fairly negative aspect of the cause of commoditization, but the evidence moved me in that direction. It's not really a conspiracy theory if it is backed up with facts.

There may be no question that the United States' workforce has been commoditized, manipulated away from the type of work that brought the United States to global superiority, leadership and example of liberty. I hope this book serves as a lesson for us and for future generations. That lesson has to do with public involvement in government, unions, education, finance and all aspects of life in the United States. I believe once you finish reading you will agree that it is likely some larger force has placed us where we are in our labor market in the United States. I am not certain of what form that force takes, or if it is a conglomerate of several different forces. But, you must agree there was an organized effort to bring us to this point. For instance, while many of us have been distracted by the "two party system", it appears at least that those two parties have found so many things in common that they have decided to work toward the elitist society which collaboration brings.

It is a fact in order to survive in the United States job market of the future you will need to do more than simply go to work and come home. Combined with shorter technology life cycles and more technology, the basic changes made in the US economy and workforce fundamentally changed the economic balance, doing away with the "middle class" as we previously knew it. When you hear talk of restoring or otherwise affecting the middle class, the discussions are not about the middle class of previous years - this is the "new middle class".

There is no doubt some of you will disagree with some of my conclusions. Unless you develop your own conclusions by seeking out this kind of information and then acting on those conclusions in some way, you will simply be one of the commoditized citizens left in a permanent reactive cycle of waiting for things to happen to you instead of making things happen. It is my opinion that the reactive life that has become the norm in the United States is what got us to the commoditized work force we are now encouraging.

In places in the book, I try to provide assistance to those who are struggling making a living in the commoditized world. Additionally in the chapters titled "How to Be a Commodity" and "How to Get Your Next Job" we will give you some tips for survival as a commodity. We may release those chapters as separate items in the future.

I look forward to hearing from you after you read and consider the commoditized phenomenon. I am sure it will open up new ideas you had not considered previously.

COMMODITIZATION VS. MONETIZATION

In order to define commoditization, one needs to understand the fundamental construction of the American economy. While commoditization is a global practice, it has had more impact on The United States for three reasons:

1) The United States has been the leader of the free world for quite a while. It has been the standard for the Free Enterprise system.

2) The United States' social system is under extreme pressure to deviate from the Constitutional Republic that has been the foundation of a Free Enterprise friendly social structure.

3) Increased economic pressures from national and international entities have introduced unknown and untested parameters into the delicate balances of free markets and capitalism.

With its free enterprise capitalist market systems, the United States is uniquely situated and has markets that did not originally operate similar to other countries.

Many have labored under this free enterprise system for generations without ever considering the unique and almost perfect system that allowed it to exist. As the core of a socio-economic system, we took for granted that all the parts worked in perfect harmony. Most of us never thought that someone or something might want to upset that system, take advantage or systematically disassemble it.

Let's take a look at the design and what came apart. Then we will discover who had a part in commoditization, and the possible reasons they did what they did.

On one end of the spectrum is labor monetization. Monetized labor is the pure conversion of labor to money. In general, being monetized assumes there is no direct competition for the labor being monetized.

On the other end is labor commoditization. Commoditized labor is the conversion of unique individual labor to a generic product. In this case, the competition is nearly perfect; the commoditized labor is so generic as to be indistinguishable from any other labor.

First we need to define the two ends of the labor value spectrum – monetization and commoditization. Monetization has the role of adapting non-revenue generating assets to generate revenue. Commoditization has the role of making goods that have economic value into simple commodities in the market.

In a purely capitalist society, it has been said that labor is commoditized and money is monetized. In a socialist society, the opposite occurs – labor is monetized and money becomes the commodity. At first, this appears to be opposite what the world would expect. Being monetized simply sounds like a capitalist condition.

Consider with me the state of "normal" in The United States. The "normal" that is the United States as described and defined in The United States Constitution.

That Constitution defines The United States of America as a Constitutional Republic. The U. S. Constitution is a contract between the fifty states in which the states agree to engage a federal government only for the purposes stated in the preamble to the Constitution: "establish justice, insure domestic tranquility, provide for the common defense, promote the general welfare, and secure the blessings of liberty to ourselves and our posterity,"

The United States began as a country dedicated to an individual's right to self-determination. To many, this is a right to agency, the ability to choose one's own path and, arguably, one's destiny.

As this government was formed, and as citizens exercised their right to agency, the free enterprise system emerged. This system, in it's root, is subject to the law of supply and demand; in particular when it comes to pricing of goods and services. The system is critical to the capitalist economic system, which is a social system based on the principle of individual rights.

There is a considerable amount of material available regarding the differences between monetization and commoditization, particularly regarding human resources and their time. I encourage you to take the time to understand the differences between the two concepts.

While one could argue that agency emanates from a divine principle founded on Christianity, this argument sometimes becomes a distraction from the discussion. Legally it is a system of objective laws (rule of law as opposed to rule of man). Economically, when such freedom is applied to the sphere of production its result is the free-market.

FREE ENTERPRISE AND CAPITALISM

Free Enterprise can be defined as "a system in which private businesses are able to compete with each other with little control by the government".

This seems a fairly simple, and logical, approach. Establish commerce without interference from government. The very essence of a nation founded in liberty.

As the definition is expanded, however, we begin to see a pervasive theory that government needs to be involved: "freedom of private business to organize and operate for profit in a competitive system without interference by government beyond regulation necessary to protect public interest and keep the national economy in balance"

Note the injection of terms such as "regulation", "protect public interest", and "economy". This begins the pervasive involvement of government into the free enterprise system. What will they regulate? Who is "the public", and what part of the economy will they keep in balance?

Let's also look at the definitions of capitalism:

The simple definition?

Capitalism – "a way of organizing an economy so that the things that are used to make and transport products (such as land, oil, factories, ships, etc.) are owned by individual people and companies rather than by the government"

Merriam Webster expands it's definition:

"an economic system characterized by private or corporate ownership of capital goods, by investments that are determined by private decision, and by prices, production, and the distribution of goods that are determined mainly by competition in a "free market". In this description, also from Merriam Webster, we see that capitalism is the result of "strong national states" (government) putting in infrastructure sufficient to support capitalism through free enterprise.

So what has happened? We can see from the descriptions of free enterprise and capitalism that the lack of government leaves the system to adjust based only on market forces. What many refer to as "the law of supply and demand" is in its pure form the only driver necessary to control production, price, cost, materials and design of products in a consumer based free enterprise system. The United States has enjoyed the unique position of being the primary consumer base for retail products. Today, the United States provides a considerable percentage of the world's consumer sales. Shrinking as a part of total world consumer demand, the United States has become part of a larger collective as consumerism has been exported to the rest of the world. For instance, in 2013, China overtook the U. S. in e-commerce for the first time in history.

The North American Free Trade Agreement (NAFTA) began a change in The United States in the early to mid-1980s. Arguing that a "free trade" agreement between countries on the North American continent (largely The United States and Mexico and Canada), proponents of the treaty saw expanding markets and options as they encouraged these free trade agreements.

One could argue this was the beginning of a new wave of "crony capitalism". The prevalence of crony capitalism has become a primary corruptor in the relationship between business, government and labor as the parties abandoned previously defined standards in the name of financial opportunity and power.

The North American Free Trade Agreement removed conventional barriers to trade within nations, opting instead for expanded access to populations in other countries. I suggest the timing of NAFTA relative to a new found (or at least more overt) dislike of unions in the United States was not coincidental. Businesses realized that in order to expand markets they needed to produce their products for less money – and foreign countries were there to provide that cheaper labor. In the process of exporting goods, the United States was importing the idea that labor cost was driven by markets – and not by the person providing the labor. This was the beginning of the commoditization of the labor market.

That idea is the basis for the commoditization of everything in the United States. Consider the reasons the world has for manipulating the United States into a position in line with a single world government – and what this means to the future of the United States.

Then consider with me what the impact is to you and your family – and what you can do to develop skills and strategies that allow you and your family to survive.

Prepare to be surprised when you realize you cannot trust government to defend the unique ideas of the American dream. Be prepared to realize that the United States government, in its never ending pattern of negotiation, has negotiated away the very government which makes that possible.

Be prepared to conclude that the ever popular term

“bipartisanship” has brought about commoditization of almost everything in the United States – including middle class workers. I will offer suggestions for near term strategies for managing the careers of your family, friends and peers. You may be surprised to find yourself advocating for political activism and involvement. I suggest the continued advocacy of the foundational behavior that began this country – an adherence to conservative principals, family, and the conventional definition of work, and a higher moral and ethical standard for us all may be our last hope to eliminate complete commoditization in The United States. You will also hear me advocate for positive attitude. “Can’t never did anything”.

Roles of men and women in commoditized society

I am certain this book will help you to discover what it takes to continue to take care of your family:

If you are in a “conventional” family, I encourage you to work hard to defend your position. Nothing is a more honorable pursuit than that of parent, child, or family member. Parents working together to raise a family are becoming more rare. Some even view parenthood as obsolete or unnecessary. If you are comfortable as a stay at home mother, then stick with it. Parenthood and marriage are very rewarding experiences.

If you are a single parent – of either gender – I know you have lots of things to worry about. This book will be of extreme importance to you as you look for ways out of the government imposed “philosophy of can’t”. Choose to be a parent and example to your children. The rewards are great.

If you are young, you need to recognize that much of what you have learned or been told is simply not true. I leave it to you to determine if these are deliberate lies, lies of ignorance or lies of omission, but I propose they are lies nonetheless. Question authority. Ask why. Develop your own opinions and goals – don't ride on someone else's goals!.

Please read the book and then go about the hard work of taking care of yourself, your family and those who will come after you. The United States – and the world – have become hardened places and provide difficult challenges at every turn.

Ask questions – this book will help you know what to ask – then start to hold people, corporations and governments accountable. In this country you have the right to ask questions. If something seems unfair or otherwise not correct, ask why !

The United States is a divine nation that has stood up for the average citizen. The commoditization of US citizens has changed almost everything about the country.

Knowing you have been Commoditized – and why - will be the first stage in knowing how to survive into the future. I wish you luck. Enjoy the book!

Chapter 1

You Have Been Commoditized!

YOUR "NORMAL" LIFE

You wake up every day to the sound of the same old thing, of the world changing. You live a fairly "normal" life, if there is such a thing anymore. You get up in the morning, go through your morning routine and prepare to face another day. In many cases, you get up at night living the inverted lifestyle of a second or third shift worker.

If you are fortunate enough to be employed, you go to work every day. You are mindful of the fact that many people do not have employment and think often of life in that situation. On most days, you arrive on time – maybe even a little early - and put in a full day performing the tasks for which you get paid. On many days, you skip or take a short lunch. You go home every day after at least an eight hour shift – although many days you work more than eight hours. You commute between thirty minutes and an hour one way, putting in at least an hour of "dead time" sitting in a car. You feel like part of the herd; dodging in and out of traffic, praying your car will hold together and that you will not be involved in an accident.

Every day, you arrive home after a hard day at work. Whether you perform manual labor, work in an office, or provide specialized services and tasks, you put a sincere one hundred percent effort in exchange for your compensation. This, of course, assumes your work requires one hundred percent of your effort.

Occasionally, you work on your personal finances, usually centered around an agreement you have negotiated to exchange your labor and/or skills for compensation. Some would say you have negotiated a "fair wage". Whether it is fair or not is sometimes up for interpretation. With the changes in the US and international labor markets, you worry often about your ability to provide for those who depend on you. With the changes in the US in general, you wonder about the financial impact of these changes on your life.

You constantly look at your personal living arrangements. Some of you feel fortunate, even blessed to have gotten where you are in your life. Many of you rent your home, apartment or other dwelling. Some of you have purchased a home. Some of you think you have purchased a home, but are beginning to realize you are renting a home from the mortgage company.

While this book is written for a world audience, this applies more to those who have the liberty to choose how they live. You know that living in America comes with the liberty to choose a freedom not available in many places in the world.

You have begun to realize you have become a consumer in the purest sense of the term. You have a nice automobile to drive, maybe two? But you are realizing that owning a car is much like owning a home. The definition of "own" has changed; much like your home, you may be simply renting your car. You buy everyday items on credit. Sometimes, you buy your groceries daily because you just aren't sure how much cash you have from day to day.

CONSUMERISM

The consumerism continues. You dine out regularly. Your home is furnished with nice furnishings.

Many of you grew up in much more meager circumstances. Your home is at least twice as large as the one in which you grew up. To go with that, you have a debt load that is twice as large as that of your parents.

Your wardrobe is fairly adequate and you seem to always have plenty to wear. Your personal technology is only one or two life cycles from the most recent technology and you feel fairly confident you are "keeping up with the Joneses" on the consumer goods.

Your entertainment budget is not enormous. But you do get out fairly often, attending a ball game, a concert, or a new movie on a regular basis. You realize you enjoy a life full of leisure activities. Regardless of your income or education, you are becoming aware that all of these things are becoming less permanent.

You watch as some of your peers aren't around as much. You feel the pain and fear of the loss of a home, either personally or through the experience of friends and peers. You notice others seem to have escaped the pain of these things, but neither you nor they have any idea why. You hope and pray that your life will not include such difficulty.

As you become more aware of the reality of this new life, you realize the life you expected is not the life you are going to have. Not because you failed in some way, but because it seems the rules have changed. Your life is going to be different, much different, than your parents. Two incomes are now required in most homes. Society expects mothers to be in the workplace, not in the home. Even if you choose, the American Dream is no longer in your reach.

You have made your share of mistakes. Some have been costly, others have simply been inconveniences. You like to believe you have learned lessons from them all. In some cases, you have run head first into a legal system that feels more like it is interested in your money than in your safety, or in true justice.

You are beginning to ask yourself about your future, all the usual questions. Will I have a job five years from now? Will I be able to provide for my family? Will I ever be able to retire?

THE WAY IT WAS

You remember, or know someone who remembers, what the middle class American lifestyle was like.

You know someone who has lived the American Dream. You know many who no longer believe there is such a thing.

You remember the way you grew up or were raised. Regardless of your race, economic or social class, you recall a different moral and ethical attitude and standard. You remember being spanked, being yelled at, being grounded, maybe even getting paddled. You remember all these things, but you also feel they are the core of your beliefs and how you try to live today.

You remember a time when work mattered. And when a person worked, they were rewarded with personal security, not wealth, but security. You are aware that security is being redefined and is much more difficult to achieve... You are aware that the middle class that you grew up in or have heard about no longer exists.

THE NEW REALITY

You have been so busy trying to "get ahead" that you have ignored what has been happening all around you.

You have been one of those who agreed that Unions had too much power. You tended to agree that Unions caused the downfall of many industries, most notably the automotive industry. You have wondered about the "exorbitant" salaries and benefits of the union worker and concluded those workers "make too much money". Is it possible this was simply a diversion as we moved towards commoditization? What is the definition of "too much" in a society where most things in life are now entitlements?

You have been one of the people who felt pretty good about your savings and about your investment portfolio. You have been convinced that your Social Security insurance will not be sufficient to provide for your retirement, and somehow not been mad the system is not delivering the insurance it promised. You are wondering why you put your wages into a 401K retirement plan that may or may not provide additional security, but definitely is out of your control.

You are one of those people who feel good about buying things you believe you need from retailers who bring all their products in from another country, and pay sub standard wages to their employees. Even though you could probably do without most of those items, you choose to frequently "pay less, live better", even if that means you have to ignore the news that thousands of people die in manufacturing facilities throughout the world in order to produce the products you buy. [1]

You continue to be a consumer of almost everything you can get your hands on. You openly wonder about whether you really need this "stuff", but don't want to deprive yourself or your family from that sixty inch LCD TV they so desperately "need". Despite the fact that you know people that were laid off from the manufacturing plant that used to make those consumer items in your home city or state, you buy them knowing that it is made in a country that is opposed to the United States, or is at least supporting treatment of workers that the United States stopped a century ago. Was this simply more diversion? Maybe........

---

[1] http://www.theguardian.com/world/2013/jun/23/rana-plaza-factory-disaster-bangladesh-primark

WHERE IS THE FUTURE?

It is hard to determine where the future is. What you will recognize is that the United States has been shipping jobs, lots of jobs, to other countries. You have been told that America is transitioning from a manufacturing economy to a service economy. You are not really sure you agree with or understand that concept, but you have left it to the "experts" to tell you the truth on the subject.

Where is the future? In its current form, the future, at least of American labor, appears to be in the hands of interests outside the United States. A commoditized labor market is the result. Remember, the conventional middle class is now non existent. Why the diversions? Some special interests don't want you to think about it........

WHAT IS THE FUTURE?

The future is full of the uncertainty that caused you to begin thinking about it. It may be the reason you purchased this book. It is the thing that keeps you awake many nights as your career is being changed, largely with you having no power to stop the change.

What is the future? There are many factors. American domestic policy seems to be not very well defined. As mentioned earlier, there are some who feel America is moving from a manufacturing economy to a service economy. There are just as many who believe the effort to move to a service based economy is not wise. What is clear is that the innovation and leadership that has caused

American success in history – Henry Ford and the production line, Bill Gates and Steve Jobs in technology, etc, seems to be waning, maybe even deliberately discouraged.

Opportunities are everywhere for a "new" American initiative. Certainly, innovation in energy, medicine and the environment are long overdue. I don't believe for a second that the gasoline powered car is the final resting place of personal transportation. At least, not in its current form using a carbon based fuel. I say this not as an activist environmentalist, but as a proud American who is amazed at what has been accomplished so far.

What is the future? It is unknown. But it is in the hearts and minds of at least two generations of Americans, waiting to be unleashed when conditions are favorable. Our duty as American citizens is to protect the liberties and security that allow us to be innovators and influencers of the future. The future is simply so bright, it is difficult to conceive.

COMMODITIZED

When you put all this information together and search for answers, you come to the unfortunate conclusion that you are more unsure of your career than ever.

As you consider your future and your choices, you are unsure of many things.

As you look at your career, you are curious as to how you can stay alive in a world where your skills, labor and time are not valued, maybe no longer needed. If we are changing from a production based society to a service based society, but you make your living producing something, what will you build? If you are converting from building to servicing, what will you service? At some point, if you are not building, what will be left to service?

When you get over the shock of it all, I have news for you. YOU are a Commodity, a mere piece of fruit, a loaf of bread, a roll of toilet paper. Your skills are simply catalogued with everyone else. You no longer have control over your career, your time or the value associated with each of them. Retail America has commoditized everything, including the human beings who made this country what it is.

With that knowledge, you need to know how to survive. This book will certainly suggest how you may do that.

However, you will be haunted by a need to know what caused your commoditization.

Stick with us through the rest of this book as we reveal what happened – and how you survive!

Chapter 2

Finance

The finance industry and its influence across cultural, ethnic and economic classes continues to be a major driving force in the world. Those forces are, quite frankly, not very patriotic towards the United States. Consider these entities one at a time and see if you agree that worldwide finance has played a large part in diminishing the value of both the working and middle classes in the United States. Each of them has played a role or had an interest in the commoditization of the American workforce.

BANKS

Banks (and bankers) have been involved in the world for much of its history. Certainly much of what they have done has been very good. In the creation of our open market, capitalist society, banks have been the funding engine for capitalism once those who used personal wealth to fund it either stopped funding it or became owners of banks.

Like all things, there have been times when bankers and other financial entities have not been truthful or transparent about their motivation.

We have seen usurious financial deals throughout the history of the world. Usury is defined as the loaning of money for unusually high rates.

At one time, it was common for the servant class to spend their lives paying off a meager debt that could never be paid (servitude), even upon their death. It can be argued that debt once again is threatening the American citizen. Tax debt, student loan debt and other bank debt have become prevalent burdens on some citizens. In the case of student loans and taxes, there is no legal relief. Even in the case of a proven inability to pay the debt, bankruptcy courts have no power to provide relief.

We have seen this a few times in American history. Tennessee Ernie Ford speaks to one form of this in his song "Sixteen Tons". In it, he speaks to his owing "my soul to the company store". In the early days of labor, particularly in Appalachia, coal miners were subject to many oppressive treatments, not the least of which was an archaic system of financing basic needs for an employee, essentially making the employee a "slave" to the practice. I propose this was an extreme form of financial oppression that occurs even today. Consider title loans, payday loans and other finance mechanisms which may charge from 300% to 600% interest on some weekly loans. Fees and charges weigh heavily on those who can afford them the least. In many cases, a simple ten dollar mistake can cost a person tens, possibly hundreds of dollars, as banks collect their fees.

OUT OF SIGHT.....

The financial interests involved in banking operate largely under the radar, looking toward opportunities to make money on the money they control. While the previous mention of banks is about the impact of finance on the worker, there are similar forces at work in every aspect of the commoditization of labor.

The commoditization of labor has many things in common with the commoditization of money. Think of the financier who looks at his money and decides there is more opportunity to make money by investing it in a foreign interest or country. For instance, Bill Gates has invested multiple millions of dollars in foreign companies and production facilities.[2]

He also spends multiple millions of dollars advocating massive social change in The United States by funding efforts to indoctrinate the children of The United States[3]. Common Core, regardless of how you view it, is a system of assimilation. In that process, he undermines the basic structure of The United States, and makes a large profit for his former company Microsoft[4]. Still unconvinced? What if I told you one of his partners was The

---

[2] http://wire.kapitall.com/investment-idea/top-10-holdings-of-cascade-investment/

[3] http://www.washingtonpost.com/politics/how-bill-gates-pulled-off-the-swift-common-core-revolution/2014/06/07/a830e32e-ec34-11e3-9f5c-9075d5508f0a_story.html

[4] http://www.washingtonpost.com/blogs/answer-sheet/wp/2014/07/12/how-microsoft-will-make-money-from-common-core-despite-what-bill-gates-said/

Chinese Government? [5]

Think of the financier who chooses to finance a business in a foreign country where labor is treated poorly. There are any number of facilities in China and in India where workers produce consumer products for pennies compared to organized cultures. One might say "capitalism knows no boundaries". But what about the jobs these people perform? What is done to fill in the holes left in The United States when these jobs disappear? What of the thousands (yes – thousands) of foreign workers who are killed in manufacturing facilities in foreign countries producing consumer goods? Who is accountable? [6]

Consider home mortgages. As more of the American population began to buy homes (that might be out of their reach), bankers are more than happy to provide financing. Using "creative" methods, bankers made money on all of these loans – sometimes taking advantage of a person's willingness to sign up for a mortgage they clearly wanted, but may not need, to purchase a home they could not afford.

BANK FEES

The finance industry famously made money on home mortgages

---

[5] http://www.gatesfoundation.org/Media-Center/Press-Releases/2011/10/Foundation-and-China-Partner-to-Address-Global-Development-Needs

[6] http://www.usatoday.com/story/news/world/2013/05/09/bangladesh-factory-collapse-death-toll/2149189/

through unscrupulous behavior. On the banks, there are many examples of ponzi schemes[7], predatory lending[8], and other factors[9].

One of the larger issues once again shows the devastation of government intervention in free enterprise. The requirement of banks to lend to those who were not qualified (or at least under qualified) created an entire division of lenders willing to manipulate borrower's applications, employment and even home values in an effort to qualify borrowers for loans it was clear they could not pay.

The examples of financial oppression and abuse run throughout American society. It is true many have emerged unscathed when they work hard, manage their finances well and avoid the perils of life. When that happens, banks and finance institutes give the appearance of being commodities. However, many have not enjoyed the benefits of hard work financial management or of the luck that allows some to avoid peril. In those cases, the financial system is there to profit from their poor choice or their bad luck.

Banks also engage in unscrupulous behavior when it comes to fees and other services. The popular insufficient funds (NSF) fee gave

---

[7] http://www.nytimes.com/2013/04/29/opinion/cracking-down-on-predatory-lending.html

[8] http://www.naca.net/issues/predatory-lending

[9] http://www.responsiblelending.org/mortgage-lending/research-analysis/unfair-and-unsafe-countrywide-white-paper.pdf

way to the overdraft fee, acknowledging that the banks and financial vendors were converting from the punitive fees charged for spending money that was not in the account to the commoditized version where charging for the overdraft was simply a product.

These fees on a person's checks or withdrawals turn those transactions into usurious coverage fees. In 2007, a report by the Center for Responsible Lending, it was noted consumers were paying fees of $17.5 billion annually on automatic overdraft loans of $15.8 billion per year.[10]

In addition, banks had use a questionable method of paying larger transactions first, causing a single overdraft to balloon into five, six, even ten opportunities for the bank to charge those fees[11].

In 2011, two banks, Citi and Wells Fargo, began processing checks from smallest to largest as a result of consumer advocates efforts to reverse that trend.[12] Still, the billions of dollars in revenue generated by these fess is enticing to financial institutions.[13]

Consider also the amortized loan, another unscrupulous tool of

---

[10] http://www.bankrate.com/finance/investing/fdic-study-outrageous-overdraft-fees-1.aspx

[11] http://articles.baltimoresun.com/2010-08-17/business/bs-bz-ambrose-pnc-overdraft-20100817_1_overdraft-fees-biggest-transactions-first-banks-process

[12] http://www.creditcards.com/credit-card-news/bank-check-processing-order-avoid-debit-overdraft-1271.php

[13] http://www.creditcards.com/credit-card-news/bank-check-processing-order-avoid-debit-overdraft-1271.php

banks that allows them to get paid first; even before paying the principal on a loan. The deceptive name is “amortization”. Unlike a simple interest loan where the interest is paid in a prorated method along with the principal, the amortized loan pays the interest first. This means that unless the loan is paid subject to the full loan term, say 30 years for a mortgage, the net effective percentage rate can be considerably higher. Amortized loans do not allow equity to grow as fast and, if they are refinanced often,, reset the borrower back to a pattern of committing a higher percentage of their payment to the payment of interest than to the payment of principle (or equity). This raises the likelihood that a person will not technically own their home for a period often longer than 30 years.

Bankers hold some sort of social responsibility while they make money selling money. Their singular focus on finance and profit may have put them in a position to help commoditize the American workforce by their contributing to the financing of a raised standard much of the middle class simply cannot afford.

RETIREMENT FUNDS

Unions had a very large hold on workforce retirement funds for quite some time. Most of the rank and file saw the value of saving. Unions saw the value of control that came with the funds. At some point, the larger companies got into the retirement fund business as well. Then bankers and the government decided this gave other people too much group power and wrote a tax law (401K) that encouraged individual retirement investment and planning. Retirement Funds, for a long time controlled by laborers and the "working class" in The United States, were gigantic and lucrative. These funds became a very large source of money for the finance community. The government once again used the tax code to create a special exemption for those electing to invest money in those accounts.

Unlike insurance, these investment and retirement accounts were funded primarily with the earner's income, some before taxes, some after. Often, taxes were deferred on some portion of those retirement donations in order to encourage the middle class to invest there.

The promise was that the investments would be "safe" and that companies would no longer control a person's retirement. The issue became that while much of the nation no longer depended on their employer to fund their retirement, each individual became responsible for their own retirement. (One of the cases where the American citizens were systematically "split up".) This was the beginning of the commoditization of retirement funds.

This theory works okay so long as the employee can afford to fund their retirement account, the economy is stable, the employee has very few periods of unemployment and the funds perform well. It also depends on a trustworthy manager of the funds. In too many cases, more than one of these conditions did not exist.

In addition, when these funds behaved independently they were viewed as competitors by other financial entities. So much so that banks began purchasing the funds in order to maintain control of where the money was invested. The conflict of interest is fairly obvious. From bankrate.com:

PENSION ABUSE WIDESPREAD

By Barbara Whelehan · Bankrate.com
Friday, September 16, 2011

Last week the nation's third-largest public pension fund announced it had established a pension abuse reporting hotline. The California State Teachers' Retirement System's new hotline enables anyone to anonymously report cases of suspected pension abuse, such as incidents of "pension spiking." That's a slick retirement planning maneuver practiced by some public-sector employees to work overtime in the years before retirement so they can get much bigger pension checks.

But what about the pension abuses that occur routinely in the private sector -- abuses that benefit the sponsoring companies but hurt their workers? I'm referring to the abuses exposed in "Retirement Heist: How Companies Plunder and Profit from the Nest Eggs of American Workers" by award-winning Wall Street Journal reporter Ellen Schultz.

RETIREMENT CRISIS

Schultz says the gradual decline of traditional pension plans has little to do with the pig-in-the-python demographic trend of baby boomers all retiring at once. She blames the retirement crisis on top executives, benefits consultants and others in the retirement industry who "played a huge and hidden role in the death spiral of American pensions and benefits."

They have not been held to account for it, she says, and, "if anything, they are viewed as beleaguered captains valiantly trying to keep their overloaded ships from being sunk in a perfect storm. In reality, they're the silent pirates who looted the ships and left them to sink, along with the retirees, as they sailed away safely in their lifeboats."

Her provocative words are backed by scathing accounts of how hundreds of large companies deliberately and deceptively cut back the pension and retiree health care benefits of the rank and file while improving their own bottom lines and the pension benefits of company executives.

CASH BALANCE PLANS

Case in point: Over the last couple of decades, hundreds of companies have frozen their pensions and converted them to cash balance plans. These are a rip-off to older employees because they end up with a much smaller benefit.

While employers can't take away the benefits that have accrued to workers, they can stop or slow the growth by freezing their plan or adopting a different formula. In other words, they change the rules. With traditional pensions, a worker's benefit grows at a much faster rate in the final working years before retirement because the formula is based on a worker's tenure and the average salary over the last few years of employment. Under cash balance plans, pensions freeze and begin growing at a slower, static rate.

That may not be news, but this was to me: At some companies, when the pensions were converted, the employees' new account balances were actually reduced. Schultz explains what happens during the conversion process.

"For example, if at the time of the pension change someone had earned the equivalent of a $300,000 payout, the opening account balance might be only $250,000. Consequently, it could take years for the pay credits to build the 'balance' back up to where it had been when the pension change was made. As a result, following the change to a cash balance plan, the pensions of older workers were frozen --- in some cases for the rest of their careers. Employees didn't notice because the amounts on their 'account statements' always appeared to be growing."

How could companies get away with this if pension law protects workers from reduced benefits? Schultz says cash balance plans got around the prohibition against retroactive pension cuts by giving employees who leave the company "at least the value of the benefit they had when the pension was changed." But those who stay on and then retire end up with greatly reduced pension payouts.

READ MORE: HTTP://WWW.BANKRATE.COM/FINANCING/RETIREMENT/PENSION-ABUSE-WIDESPREAD/#IXZZ2WPF8AHC3

GOVERNMENT

Government entities have always been motivated by financial interests, many of which have ulterior motives, sometimes corrupted. One could say they have been bought out of the "business of government". Government – which should not be "for profit", finds itself competing financially with private business for financial gain. Banks, payday loan companies, securities and bond traders and many others all continue to lobby Congress for special treatment by the IRS. These exemptions have prerequisites that motivate a certain behavior which generally benefits the financial entities. There are many new “vehicles” for profit and those vehicles have been the beneficiaries of government taxation and regulation in their favor.

Regulatory authority is written and executed to favor financial entities throughout the country in exchange for something the government wants to require. Regulators work to ensure the financial institutions work within the rules set up to require a certain behavior.

Finally, some people get involved in illegal and or unethical behavior, cheating the system in the name of profit. Examples of corrupt government employees abound as the country spirals in current times.

CRONY CAPITALISM

It should come as no surprise that individuals have become corrupted by the system. As you will read, participants in the commoditization of the United States’ labor market come from a variety of industry, finance and government institutions.

Crony capitalism is a term describing an economy in which success in business depends on close relationships between business people and government officials. It may be exhibited by favoritism in the distribution of legal permits, government grants, special tax breaks, or other forms of state interventionism.

This crony capitalism comes when the person decides he has a price – and then someone is willing to pay the price. Regardless of political affiliation, government officials are enticed monetarily to make a specific law pass or fail, ensure a project gets funded, or to ensure a specific person or group get favorable treatment. When the politician chooses thie influence over the direction received from constituents, it is reasonable to suspect that crony capitalism contributed to those events.

THE WORLD

While the United States enjoys a unique economy built to encourage success, security and happiness, much of the world does not. Whether this is due to the form of government, external or internal conditions in that country, or even crony capitalism, the uniqueness of the United States' economic system is seen as an opportunity to take advantage in the name of money.

Nations, corporations and individuals throughout the world have taken the opportunity whenever possible to invest in or do business with American entities. From China to Microsoft to George Soros, these world influencers have taken on the role of participant, even protagonist for the United Nations' one world government plans. In addition, the jealousy many foreign countries feel toward the U. S. causes them to be participants in global efforts to do harm to the United States. Whether it is through mortgage loans, consumer goods or government interference, the stated goal is always to do harm and bring the country down through economic means.

Just look at China. This country contributes to commoditization because it is in China's best long-term interest to de-stabilize the United States. It has done that by infiltrating the American markets through cheap labor, cheap money and cheap products. It has also done that by encouraging American investors to invest their money in China based projects. This takes investment money out of the United States, relocates manufacturing to China, and further erodes the employment formerly counted on to support the American middle class.

China is not alone in these efforts. India, Pakistan, Japan, Korea and many others are systematically eroding the security of the American middle class. Combined with the efforts of many consumer level retailers and the availability of products over the Internet, the relocation of manufacturing, financed by worldwide financial leaders, has virtually guaranteed the commoditization of American workers.

With the UN's help, many world powers are benefitting from the downgrading of the American workforce. As a part of a much larger plan to bring the entire world under one government, the New World Order has been titled Agenda21.[14]

RETAIL

The commoditization of the United States' labor market is a direct reflection of the commoditization of everything else in the world.

---

[14] http://www.theblaze.com/stories/2012/11/19/what-is-agenda-21-after-watching-this-you-may-not-want-to-know/

Of all the things that may be commoditized, a person's time may be the last remaining thing available.

When I was raising my first family, I discussed the prioritization of my life with a very wise man. He introduced me to a concept that I try to remember always: "You may always make more money, but you may never make more time". This maxim perfectly illustrates the importance of time management. How many people are willing to do almost anything for money? How many people view low price as the ultimate motivator? What is the impact of "save money, live better" on the labor force ?

In the world of retail everything has an assigned value, shelf life and place in the store. In the high volume/low margin retail system, everything has been commoditized to the extreme. Human resources are often treated similarly to these retail commodities. Take, for instance big (and some small) box workers, who spend their very limited hours in the pursuit of whatever tasks they are employed to accomplish. As commoditized workers, these employees are reduced to extreme non-skilled status and are limited in their hourly rate, number of hours worked, benefits and, in some cases, opportunities to break out of the cycle.

CAPITALISM

Capitalism is considered to be unique to the United States, and for awhile, was a sort of export from the United States. It may surprise some to find out that commoditized labor is the normal condition for labor in a capitalist society. In capitalism, the normal conditions are that money is the constant and labor is commoditized. In pure socialism, labor is monetized and money is the commodity.

I discovered this situation as I did the research for this book. It appears that commoditized labor is the norm in capitalism but that unions and organized labor historically kept that condition from occurring in the United States. With this in mind, it is no wonder that unions have been reduced. It should be noted that unions do not appear to have been aware this was one of the reasons their influence has been so reduced.

This would be why commoditization has come along later in the cycle. It could be that this is a natural consequence of the more recent open disdain for unions and organized labor. As these groups became less popular as they got a little out of control (some might say a lot out of control) late in the last century, and as the Democratic Party, once the party of labor, turned its back on labor, this cleared the way for commoditization of that labor.

GREED

One of the consequences of bad financial practices is greed. Surely we can see the effects of greed on the United States. “The love of money” is evil. As people, businesses and politicians became more concerned with themselves than with the general good, commoditization was the natural result.

At what point do we consider this behavior greedy? What makes a person, company, or government greedy? We asked the question previously; what is the measure of "enough?

BIG MONEY

When we discuss big money, we have to recognize the gap between the financial classes in the United States, the "haves" and "have-nots", has gotten wider. With that in mind, it must be said that the ultra wealthy are manipulating retail and wholesale markets throughout the world. They are also manipulating manufacturing in a number of ways. From deciding what gets manufactured to where it gets manufactured, these super rich only concern themselves with profit and manipulation of markets. Once again, the common good suffers.

Questions have to be asked about the likes of George Soros, who uses his billions to support a liberal leaning government in the United States. What is his motivation for manipulating entire societal classes?

We should wonder why Bill Gates would take most of his wealth, arguably made in the United States, and invest so much in the very foreign companies that helped create the commoditization about which we are learning.

Included in this list would be independently wealthy individuals like Mitt Romney, The Koch Brothers, Michael Bloomberg, and even the President of The United States. What are they doing to support the American Dream if their investments are going to foreign countries and if their money is being kept in foreign banks? This is not to say that big money should be illegal, but it is to point out that big money may not have the same goals the middle class has. The reasons for the ultra wealthy to invest outside of the United States may not be as sinister as I make it sound. With tax laws, regulations, the interference of international finance and the United Nations, one can see why a wealthy person would spend money elsewhere. However, some would say this has contributed to the commoditization of the American worker.[15]

SUMMARY

Banks and the financial industries have contributed heavily to the commoditization of the American work force. Their extreme focus on money as a commodity (profit) has distracted the American people from the need to protect the labor force that has been the foundation of the middle class in the United States.

Throughout the process of commoditization, finance has played a part. Certainly in protecting their ability to profit from the household budgets of the working class, their placing profit above sustainability is having an impact on commoditization.

The encouragement coming from financial interests to seek out the cheapest or least expensive item, regardless of the consequence, is prevalent. Marketing interests encourage people to find the least expensive option, – ignoring the quality or source of the product being purchased. But we also know that American consumers are

[15] http://www.investopedia.com/articles/02/020602.asp

not very predictable about buying the cheapest product.[16]

CONCLUSIONS

Unfortunately, we are left to conclude that banks and other financial interests, both foreign and domestic, have been engaged in a process of commoditizing labor in order to propagate their influence, thereby strengthening their ability to maximize profit. This is not to say that profit is bad. But financial interests should be more selective and careful about how they use money and profit to influence the world. In order to decrease the influence of commoditized labor, a return to focus on investment in American manufacturing may need to occur.

[16] http://conversionxl.com/pricing-experiments-you-might-not-know-but-can-learn-from/#.

Chapter 3

Corporate America

What role should corporations play in determining the workplace environment in America? This seems like a pretty obvious question. As corporations generally provide a large segment of opportunity for employment, they are one of the larger determinants of what the need is for workers, what skills are needed and how those skills are put to use.

Their unique needs are filled by workers with specialties in specific fields. General needs are filled by those who perform the underlying work necessary to run all business, from cleaning, to accounting, to management, to specialized skills in a number of industries. These resources are the basis for many businesses. The ultimate goal is to make a profit.

Let's look at corporate America and their participation in the commoditization of the workforce. At what point did corporations begin influencing the job market to their benefit? Are corporations under any obligation to treat their workforce fairly? What is appropriate behavior for a corporation, and what might not be? What forces of finance, education, labor and government become influences in a corporation's decisions about the workforce? What part does the worker play in those decisions?

GOVERNMENT REGULATION

For most of the last 200 years, American companies were competing primarily with other American companies. In the early 1900s, after labor organized into what are now known as Unions, the prevalence of those unions kept wages and benefits fairly well evened out. Safety was being vastly improved. Child labor and severe work conditions were being removed from the workplace as well. By setting the standard for wages, benefits, safety and child labor, even those workers not in unions benefited from the work of the organized union effort.

Certainly, the likelihood that a large number of workers would die in an industrial or labor force accident has been reduced as organized labor advocated for workplace safety. Whether this would have happened without organized labor cannot really be disputed.

Unfortunately, the only way their efforts could enjoy the success they have is by having the government become the enforcement arm of labor. It is unlikely that workplace safety would have gotten the attention it did, and still has, if the state and federal governments had not created offices like the Occupational Safety and Health Administration and the Department of Labor. The impact of the government on free market forces that control labor can be argued to have a negative impact if the control (regulation) becomes too onerous or tyrannical. Whether over-regulation is a root cause of commoditization is something that is still up for discussion. Whether labor outspent and outmaneuvered corporate America for a time cannot be disputed. One could argue it simply took time for corporate forces to turn the tide on the labor movement.

While unions negotiated wages, benefits and work conditions, companies naturally remained concerned with profitability. Good managers realized early on that profit was tied to productivity. They were able to achieve success and profits through more conventional management of those companies in the free market consumer economy of the United States. This included the management of all overhead, of which labor was a large piece. Referring back to the thought that labor is commoditized in a capitalist society, one can see how the current commoditization was simply delayed by this union involvement.[17]

FOREIGN INVESTMENT

It is hard to tell when, but at some point American manufacturers started to realize they could have products manufactured in other countries, and then bring them back into the United States cheaper than they could manufacture them with American labor. The United States government seemed to agree, and began to manipulate import/export laws to make that decision more tenable. Beginning in the late 1970s, there was a definitive move by corporate America to legislate a change in American manufacturing, It was an opportunity to make more money. One of the tools that emerged was titled NAFTA. It would be described in 1992 by Ross Perot, a wealthy, highly successful entrepreneur and

[17] http://barefootbum.blogspot.com/2008/12/commoditization-of-labor.html

American businessman, as a "giant sucking sound", a colorful phrase for what he believed would be the negative effects of the proposal. The phrase, coined during the 1992 U.S. presidential campaign, referred to the sound of U.S. jobs and money “heading south for Mexico” should the proposed free-trade agreement go into effect.

Was the change underway because companies were weary of the unions? Unions certainly had an impact. Were unions entirely to blame for these movements? Hardly. While unions were definitely contributing to the demise of the American manufacturing sector, there were others who would be participating as well. We will talk in depth about unions and the other factors involved later in the book.[18]

TAXES

Tax rates and other government regulation also had their impact. Ross Perot's reference to the "giant sucking sound" did not simply refer to jobs. It also applied to the movement of legislation and money. Legislation relative to the taxes, import and export fees and other levies contributed heavily to decisions about manufacturing. Money going "south of the border" became difficult to track and to monitor as Mexico did not have the controls in place that were needed to provide transparency and traceability.

As a result of the government's manipulation of the manufacturing

[18] http://www.cfr.org/trade/naftas-economic-impact/p15790

of certain goods, the profitability of a corporation was now being actively manipulated by forces largely out of the control of the company itself. This was bound to place strain on those responsible for ensuring the success of American corporations. Rather than being proactive and innovative, manufacturers and service providers in American corporations had been put in the business of reacting to outside forces, most of whom now had a direct influence on the bottom line of those corporations.
Arguably, many corporations simply moved operations or created divisions based in foreign countries. In those cases, the only thing that changed was the source of the labor. This had a very clear impact on the commoditization of the American labor market.
This situation set up what we have now, a purely reactive business environment where companies existed almost solely to produce profit; manufacturing became secondary to profit. This is a reactive and defensive stance that stifles America because it makes profit the only, or at least primary, motivator. Prior to these conditions, companies were focused on the product, how to produce it and how to make it better, now they simply looked for the profit. Along with employing a large number of American citizens and producing goods for consumption, producing a profit had always been a motivator. At some point, the profit simply garnered more attention.
Some would argue that the primary goal of American business had always been profit. While it is true that free enterprise focuses on profitability, much of the innovation and new ideas came from

people who placed as much importance on their own satisfaction as they did on the business profit. As America moved away from the mom and pop model, this emphasis on motivators other than profit has diminished, thus increasing the trend towards commoditization.

American corporations then began enlisting the assistance of advocates, many of them known as lobbyists, to advocate for the benefit of the corporation or industry. Again, manufacturing, design and innovation took second place behind the protection of profit.

Enter international markets and corporations. With their influence, many of which did not have the same standard or motivation as America, those markets began to influence profits of American companies by re-introducing the (bad?) standards America had worked so hard to eliminate. As a result, Americans saw goods produced in facilities in other countries by underage children working seven day, fourteen hour shifts. These were the same horrible conditions that American unions, corporations, and the government had worked hard to banish from the workplace in the United States. One could argue that once these conditions occurred, the playing field was out of balance. American corporations had no choice but to decide against the homeland in favor of other countries, partially because the American government was advocating for that to occur. Of course, corporations were not opposed to reduced labor costs either.

At the same time, those international markets allowed the profit motivated manufacturers to escape the onerous regulation of U. S. government departments. The EPA, OSHA, and other government functions were imposing unrealistic and crippling expectations on the manufacture of goods in the United States.

That is not to say the EPA, OSHA and others do not serve a purpose. The dumping of hazardous chemicals, for example, should never have been tolerated. Also, workers should be afforded a safe work environment. The problem is that US law has no jurisdiction in other countries. Consequently, the US Government was in effect encouraging business to go outside our borders to manufacture their products.

In 2013, we saw thousands of textile workers killed in factories where workplace safety was not a concern.[19] [20] When was the last time hundreds of workers were killed in an American factory? In India in 2013, more than a thousand workers were killed in the collapse of a manufacturing facility that made shirts and other clothing for consumption in American stores. Consider for a moment the impact if that had occurred on American soil. Now consider the tiny impact the event had because of where it occurred. One of my questions is always, "Why would anyone purchase products made under slave labor conditions, even if they could "live better"?

---

[19] http://www.bbc.com/news/world-asia-25585054

[20] http://www.huffingtonpost.com/2013/05/10/bangladesh-factory-collapse_n_3249808.html

These events are reminiscent of events such as the Triangle Shirtwaist factory in Manhattan New York fire in 1911 which killed 146 workers.[21]

In the name of profit, U.S. companies chose to get around U.S. laws and standards by simply engaging a labor force willing to work for less than five percent of the compensation of American workers. Combined with the ability to build manufacturing in foreign countries where costs are ten percent of those in America, American corporations began looking elsewhere for profits on American consumer goods.

American companies simply went elsewhere in order to protect profits. How did this happen? Why did Americans participate in this situation? A popular mantra today is "Save money, live better" No one is asking the question save money how? Or, "do I really live better?" We will talk about that later in the book.

ANTI-UNION BEHAVIOR

In the United States, we have gotten to the point where we seek vengeance and retribution as sport. There was a time when corporations took a more aggressive and open anti-union stance. Anti-union behavior is curious to me. We see it throughout the country as we discuss the root cause of commoditization with American citizens. There are many who actively avoid dealing with unions, or with companies that have unions. They boycott

[21] http://en.wikipedia.org/wiki/Triangle_Shirtwaist_Factory_fire

products made by union labor, they complain about union workers, they contribute to the general idea that unions (and by association - their members) are lazy, deceptive, produce poor quality products or services, and are paid too much money.

Yet, these same people will complain about the lack of jobs in America and in their communities. They will choose to shop at a store that sources 80% of the products it sells from a country that openly despises the United States and which has displaced the very jobs they complain about not having.

It must be argued that the loss of Unions did cause the loss of a voice for the middle class – or at least the working class. That loss at least contributed to the commoditization of the American workforce as jobs that might otherwise have remained in the United States through the protection of unions were moved because the middle class had no voice.

"OFF-SHORING" MANUFACTURING

A few years ago, at its own peril, U.S. manufacturers and corporations began to "offshore" large segments of work wherever possible. These manufacturers and corporations, and some service industries, viewed the availability of offshore labor as a boon to their businesses. When we look at profit as the primary motivator, this is an understandable reaction to the issue of labor costs.

This effort has met with great success as American consumers discovered slave labor, child labor, sub standard conditions and dangerous circumstances in many of the facilities and countries where this manufacturing was occurring. We have mentioned the deaths of thousands of workers in foreign countries. As I mention elsewhere, one has to wonder how many Americans would still look for the least expensive products if they knew people were being killed in the process of manufacturing those products.

In many cases, American manufacturers had committed the ultimate lockout, simply moving the entire operation offshore to avoid, what some would argue, was a corporate responsibility to give back to the country that allowed them their success in the first place. Whether this was good or bad, whether it contributed or did not contribute to commoditization, could be discussed at length. We must have the discussion again about whether off-shoring is a treasonous activity. If we had a percentage threshold or some other measurement beyond which manufacturing could not take their jobs out of the country, would that be protectionism?[22] The advantages and disadvantages are obvious. In the short term, competition is able to take domestic issues into account. In the long term, international competitiveness can be harmed. If trade internationally is important, this can be an issue. If, as is the case with commoditization, the cost of international competitiveness outweighs domestic interests, one would suggest a little protectionism could be a net positive. Without protectionism, commoditization is inevitable.

In the next chapter, we will discuss the government's part in this

[22] http://useconomy.about.com/od/glossary/g/Trade-Protectionism.htm

phenomenon. Their motivation would also be financial, and possibly even a little social engineering, as government's role became more authoritarian and socialist in nature. Combined with the effort of foreign governments to infiltrate American markets, and The United Nations' One World Order (Agenda 21), the government's social engineering has proven to be the source of many problems in the United States. Is it possible off-shoring is part of a larger effort to systematically dismantle the United States entirely? It would certainly appear that way.

THE US CHAMBER OF COMMERCE

The Chamber of Commerce has always been an organization with a singular focus. Their goal is always to seek out and advocate for business in America.

In 2014, it became apparent that low wages were being sought out aggressively on behalf of American business. Some argued the massive influx of "illegal" aliens was being openly tolerated by some political people because the Chamber was advocating cheap labor.

This discussion introduced the idea that crony capitalism was influencing politicians' behavior relative to labor, manufacturing and markets. This crony capitalist behavior contributed to the commoditization of American labor.

CAPITALISM AND "FREE MARKETS"

The word Capitalism is a noun defined as "An economic and political system in which a country's trade and industry are controlled by private owners for profit." When we combine this description with the fact that the United States is a Constitutional Republic, it becomes easy to see that moral and ethical behavior combined with patriotism could produce a solid demand for labor for the foreseeable future.

However, it does not take much to see this description is a double edged sword for the American way of life. Capitalism has worked, and worked well, for the entire existence of this country. In recent years, one could argue that corrupt capitalism has not been a good model for American businesses.

Our capitalist society demands many things, but none more corrupting than capitalism itself. Capitalism has motivated many to great things as they sought the fortunes deriving from turning nothing into something.

But in the wrong hands, or with the wrong mindset, or even with a sinister mind, capitalism motivates that same ingenuity in the name of evil. It also does something else; it creates the illusion and division of class. Indeed, the elitist class ceases to exist without wealth. And wealth is likely the first thing most of you think of when you think of capitalism. However, examples of the impact of corruption on corporations are everywhere. A review of Enron, Health South, any number of investment and mortgage companies and a variety of manufacturing companies will reveal unscrupulous behavior resulting in a heavy negative impact for a wide ranging population in the United States.

Capitalism is one of the primary motivators for people worldwide to come up with new ideas, and then take risks to see them become reality. It is the "engine of commerce" providing jobs, cash flow, taxes and goods for consumption. Ultimately, it is the essence of the American gross domestic product (GDP). The entire American dream was financed by capitalism. (As an overstatement of the point, and a reminder, government funding of any private enterprise is absolutely NOT capitalism.)

Why, then do so many people see capitalism as bad? It is a supreme motivator in the United States. It is the cash engine for almost every aspect of American life. If it is supreme, is there a point at which capitalism guarantees unethical, even immoral behavior? At what point does the end not justify the means in a capitalist society? I propose some American citizens see it as bad because of the corruption the behavior has bred.

Many in the United States are still advocates of capitalism. We have seen it work many times and believe it is at the core of this Nation's successes. Some are convinced that capitalism makes some parts of society less effective. Certainly we have seen when capitalism and socialism combine; we get corporatism, a sort of socialized, and elitist, prosperity that leaves a large segment of the population out of the system of capitalism.

Small business has been a large factor in the American economy and way of life. The perfect balance of free trade and capitalism in the United States makes the American dream possible. No one anywhere can beat the innovation and efficiency that has historically come from American small business. This country has been the beneficiary of a uniquely American experience, freeing individuals to pursue their "dreams". An over active government, (large taxes, high amounts of regulation, enormous oversight), kill that initiative over time.

Can free enterprise and market driven capitalism exist at the same time? In late 2013, politicians, professors, laborers, and many others were concluding these two models cannot co-exist. The question is certainly worth more time to investigate.

SUMMARY

Corporate America was once an example to the world of ethical and sound business management. As leaders in innovation, industry, manufacturing and technology, their ability to produce the Industrial Revolution, military machines, manned space exploration, and even the middle class, were well documented. The innovation coming from U.S. companies has historically proven people are limitless in their ability to conceive of, and build, marvelous things.

Free enterprise and capitalism depend on corporations to be one of the primary participants in the machine that is capitalism.

A number of conditions caused corporate America to disassemble the American workforce, or at least allow it to be disassembled. The value and importance of the American worker has been diminished in the move towards a service economy in the United States.

Corporatism, with the need for favors, exemptions and exceptions, brought corporate America into the business of needing lobbyists, hired guns to advocate for corporate America. Those relationships did not consider the impact on the American work force and contributed to commoditization. The work force has been commoditized because it also has become commoditized and secondary to the process of "making" money in the corporate world.

CONCLUSIONS

There exists a great need to remove corruption from the elitists and ruling class who run corporate America. A rediscovered dedication to America would not hurt either. Certainly, American owned corporations should get a better treatment than foreign owned interests.

A revision of the tax code would help as well. Some advocates of a restructured tax system suggest there should be no corporate tax at all, simply because the corporate tax encourages abuse of tax code at all points.

Chapter 4

American Government

The United States set the standard from which world labor forces have been measured for years. The world has looked to the United States as the example of a delicate balance.

The coexistence of forces throughout the economic, business and social classes have come together for the common good of America as a united country. Initially that balance was struck with very little influence or interference from government, certainly not from the forms of big government that have interfered in the market since the 1950s.

Certainly, there was a balance achieved between labor and business that caused industry in the U. S. to thrive. The American labor force set a standard and maintained a force that was the envy of the world.

It is difficult to point to a single event or force that caused the U.S. government to become a primary participant in the commoditization of labor. There have been clear efforts by any number of foreign and domestic entities to change the structure of the American work force. In the process of commoditization, many of those entities manipulated government in their favor, shutting out the forces that may have protected or advocated for the American worker.

Since 1980, the ongoing argument has been about the size of government and what role government should play in protecting America's interests. As government grows, its' ability to stifle free enterprise is fed by its' own voracious appetite for power and control. While that same government can artificially infuse some measure of growth, it is only brought through an infusion of massive amounts of money; money it neither owns nor has the power to control (provided you ignore the influence of the Federal Reserve). As the absolute power of government corrupts everything it touches absolutely, free enterprise is held down as an entity secondary to the government. This model has been proven through time to be unsustainable.

In the early 1900's, government was not involved in the establishment of labor policy. The markets did a fair job of establishing free market rules, prevailing wage and demand. Over time, special interests (labor, business, lobbyists) began using the court systems to try to get their way on issues. For a time, government, economists and others realized the force of government intrusion would upset the delicate balance between the parties.

It is clear that the influence of each segment covered in this book has been geared towards influencing the government to make decisions that benefit that entity. After this review, a person should be able to make up their mind about whether big government has been successful in protecting the interests of the country, or whether big government has been ineffective at those protections.

It is conceivable; the government is even actively engaged in changing the American labor force for its own interests or for the interests of the crony capitalists who run the United States government.

TAXES

What influence do taxes have on the workforce? I remember my first exposure to the concept of taxes and their real impact on the American economy. I was a union member when I first heard a radio broadcaster named Paul Harvey say “Businesses don’t pay taxes. People pay taxes”. His theory went on to say that corporations DO pay the taxes, but only after they have included those taxes in their product. Therefore, the PEOPLE pay ALL taxes.

If this is the case, then one could argue that taxation had nothing to do with the commoditization of labor. But does anyone really believe this?

Consider for a moment that the government wants a product to be produced. Would it be possible for the government to reduce or eliminate taxes on that product in order to encourage its production? Consider the converse, what if they don’t want it produced? You can see how this might impact the commoditization of labor.

What about exports and imports? Consider if the United States government wanted to steer production of a product into, or out of, the United States. Is it possible the government could actively determine where a manufacturer produces the product?

Does taxation of businesses impact business growth and jobs? Absolutely. Does the government have an agenda relative to workforces, business, labor, etc? Without question. Is it possible, even likely, the U. S. government has used tax policy to manipulate the American worker into the position of being a commodity?

Consider the total impact of taxation, federal, state, county, and city. Combine international taxation and you see a commoditized American workforce could be in the government's best interest, particularly if the workers no longer have a representative defending against such taxation.

REGULATION

What influence does government regulation have on the workforce and commoditization? Certainly since 1960, government has created a large number of agencies imposing administrative, operational and legal burdens on American manufacturing. The EPA, OSHA, NLRB and others each have become an enforcement arm of government policy regarding the full spectrum of free enterprise, often with unyielding authority and with the full ability to interfere in that free enterprise.

Have some companies acted in such a way that the agencies were needed? Possibly; but at what cost to American civilization?

Is this (regulation) the proper role of government? In a Constitutional Republic such as the United States, the role of government is to provide for the security of the nation and for the “common good”. What is the difference between providing for these things and forcing these things to occur? What if American labor needs work that one of the regulatory agencies regards as “against the law”?

Is what the regulators are doing necessary? If the United States were not a republic, for instance, if this country were a socialist or dictator regime, one might argue that government regulation could be justified. After all, the industry would belong to the government. But when free enterprise and capitalism are involved, is it possible for a government to see things clearly enough to deliver an impartial judgment as to the role of government regulation?

If it were not the government, who would do these things? Let’s remember the consumer has amazing power. If consumers were aware of the situation, they could simply choose to force the manufacturer to correct the situation through free enterprise.

Since the mid 1980’s, the United States Government has been engaged in a significant growth. Federal spending has risen. The budget deficit continues to increase. The number of individuals receiving federal assistance has grown. Police departments are being militarized. The Department of Education is dictating education standards. In almost every imaginable area, the U.S. government has been expanding at an alarming rate. Some would argue it is over reaching in many of these areas. It seems obvious that over-regulation has been driving entrepreneurship, innovation and employment out of the United States.

It is not hard to find examples of the impact of government regulation on the commoditization of the American labor market. Labor laws are onerous, demanding compliance with voluminous local and federal laws, and making the unions' demands look mild in comparison. In fact, one could conclude that putting the full force of the law behind many issues that were formerly part of a union contract helped to destroy the unions in America. Can it be that the government ultimately saw the union movement as a competitor and simply allowed it to be destroyed?

TRADE POLICIES

What influence does trade policy have on the labor market? Is it possible that foreign interests can encourage trade policies harmful to the United States labor market? Some would argue they are doing just that, and possibly harming the United States as well.

WHAT DOES THE GOVERNMENT DO ABOUT YOUR JOB?

It is sad, and probably a little paranoid, but I am afraid history shows the United States Government has always used its' citizens as pawns in multiple social engineering experiments. You can see how a move away from small government and fiscal responsibility left the government no choice but to begin manipulating the free market and the jobs that have served the country so well. As a "grand experiment", the United States government is always adjusting in the quest for more power and authority.

Even in the days leading up to and including Lincoln, the United

States government had begun to exhibit behavior similar to the oppressive government this country was created to oppose. Reading history, one can see the ongoing discussion regarding the size of government and the impact of its' role in everyday life in the country. Serious research into history will reveal many instances where the United States government, as well as the individual state governments, engaged in social manipulation, slavery, financial misdeeds and the compelling of citizens to do things they might not otherwise choose.

In his book "*IT'S OK TO LEAVE THE PLANTATION*", Mason Weaver helps us see that slavery can have many meanings to the American people. He also reveals how the government manipulated the population of the country even back in the days of slavery. The author makes a case for the possibility our government is still engaged in some form of slavery. Thus, the concept that government can get too big is revealed. Take a look at government programs in existence today. What is your faith that these programs are efficiently run and contribute to the greater good in a way that does not put a percentage of the population in permanent poverty and socialized misery?

In a constitutional republic, what DOES the government do about your job? As you will see, the less they do, the more evenly job creation occurs.

In a free society, with what are we comfortable? Is it OK for the government to reach into private business and dictate how that business runs? Is it Ok for the government to dictate that the business do something that harms the business? Is it OK for the government to mandate the purchase of a specific product? How does that influence free enterprise?

How do free markets and corporations survive? When government "takes over" how do we free the markets to act independently if they are always subject to government imposition? Moreover, what is the measure we use to tell when government has "too much" influence?

The government currently determines each of our futures by their behavior. If we are a constitutional republic, at what point is the government overreach responsible for the destruction of markets and for the commoditization of the remaining labor pool? Taxes and the exemptions that come with them, regulations, mandates, and all other regulation and manipulation of natural law all impact the profit margins of businesses throughout the country. They also impact all of our households and budgets.

What a government should do is simple. It should provide and protect the infrastructure and framework upon which businesses run. In a constitutional republic, this and security should be the primary (only?) role of government.

What a government can do is to manipulate markets by levying import and export fees such that an advantage can be found on one side or the other of a financial deal. Manufacturers are at the mercy of these policies. If the government decides to manipulate the market through taxes, fines and levies, they are manipulating the markets, thereby helping to determine how you will provide for your family.

In addition, the government can determine the level and cost of infrastructure throughout the country. This cost is supposedly written into the tax code of the states and of the federal government. Today, some advocates of big government have decided that the government should be given at least some of the credit for the success of business by virtue of their having created the infrastructure. This argument misses the point entirely. Governments cannot do anything without tax revenues. In a representative government, the citizens fund those infrastructure projects. Giving credit to the government for creating what the citizens directed be created is somewhat like billing someone for a house they already own.

As a related issue, the government can create reactionary agencies such as the EPA, OSHA and others to impede in any number of ways the manufacturing of goods throughout the country. Combined with private agencies engaged in blind restriction of human activity, these regulations and other laws create burdens on the manufacturers of goods. In some cases, the purchase of some of these items itself becomes illegal.

No one would propose that unfettered pollution, unfair labor practices, unfettered abuse of animals and all the other "bad" behaviors big government is trying to legislate away is something we want to have in this country. However, it must be recognized that many of these agencies act only upon the United States and not on other countries. Consequently, simply moving a manufacturing plant from Texas to Mexico could remove significant restrictions from an operating business. Moving jobs from the United States to India fundamentally changes the bottom lines of businesses while also obliterating entire segments of manufacturing in the United States. Has American law kept these changes from happening? Just look at the thousands of garment workers killed in India while producing clothing to be sold in the United States to find we have simply regulated these industries into moving to a country where fair labor practices do not exist. Citizens of those countries have no rights. So, the United States government is supporting the oppression of another nation's citizens in the name of consumerism, and commoditizing labor by moving those jobs to a foreign country.

In the 1980's, the United States had enrolled in NAFTA. It is reasonable to expect that the U. S. government was writing tax and import/export law to benefit NAFTA; not so. There existed an attitude of justification for the government's involvement in micro-managing the opportunities on both sides of the border. Ross Perot's "giant sucking sound" was correct; jobs and money were going south of the border. This would commoditize labor even further.

Combine that with the unrealistic approach being used by agencies such as the Environmental Protection Agency and one can understand how some feel the country has clearly become unfriendly to business. Whether global warming is real or not, the fact is that the human race is on the planet and uses its resources to support the populace. Onerous regulation and overstepping by government agencies have frightened manufacturers, and in some cases, run them out of business in the name of compliance. How ridiculous is it that we have regulation prohibiting manufacturing processes, but the company can move to a foreign country just south of the U. S. border and freely perform that operation without any ability to continue the regulation. Arguably, our government has encouraged that part of manufacturing to leave the United States.

Is it possible for man to live on the planet without some sort of impact on the biosphere? If the answer is no, then how do we measure the impact, and is that impact always "bad"? The U. S. Government has allowed over regulation to contribute to the commoditization of the workforce, and to reduce the standard of living of everyone throughout the world in the process.

THE UNITED NATIONS?

In many open forums on the subject of national interest, you will find the U. S. government is actively working to limit manufacturing within its own borders. It is remarkable to watch and listen to these forums where opponents of American manufacturing call efforts to bring manufacturing back to this country protectionism. Every country on earth engages in some level of protecting their own markets, but the United States gets blamed for proposing "protectionist" policies benefiting their own country.

The U. S. should be engaged in protecting its own interests.

Arguably, commoditization has proven to be bad for the country. Diminishing the importance of a closed loop free market system in a capitalist country helps to sell the idea that all things are equal and that the U. S. cannot isolate itself from the world. I propose this just feeds the globalization efforts of groups like the United Nations.

The U. S. has been a member of the United Nations since its inception. Many do not feel this is in the country's best interest. If labor commoditization is part of the United Nations' plan for a One World Order (Agenda 21), it is understandable. In their efforts to force the world to live under a single government, it is necessary to level the playing field. With labor rates, regulation and taxes so much different (arguably better) in the U. S., the only way the One World Order (Agenda 21) works is to systematically disassemble it.

Consider also the fact that the government has failed to do the one thing it is chartered by the Constitution to do; provide security. The borders of the United States are supposed to be secured by the government. We know the government has failed in that effort. Globalization is a United Nations effort which is being subversively pushed into the United States. It is unfortunate that many big money, big politics and big banking players (Bill Gates, George Soros, Barack Obama, the Clintons, the Bushes and many others) have been agents of globalization in their investments, their efforts to provide aid and in their politics. Globalization is not exclusive to any party or philosophy. The consequence of globalization is the commoditization of all people in order to make them all feel as if they are equal. The problem is that all people become equally commoditized.

What is the government's motivation to simply ignore aliens coming across the United States' borders? Could it be a part of the plan to simply open the doors and encourage the dilution of American workers? When judged in the terms of globalization, this invasion is a deliberate effort to commoditize American workers.

In 2014, some members of the Republican Party began to look at Crony Capitalism as it relates to government policy, particularly in relation to the influx of illegal aliens through the southern U. S. border. As they looked at this cronyism, it became apparent the U. S. Chamber of Commerce was in a conflict of interest. The Chamber may have been blinded by greed and allowed their need for cheap labor to overtake their sense of loyalty to business and the general health of the United States. Those discussions have become a part of the discussion about the root cause of the insecure border to the south.

The question is "What does the government do about your job?" It is sad to think they do more than you think, most of which is not to the benefit of taxpaying American citizens. This is simply more reason to pay attention and be immersed in the political process. The government is doing far more to remove employment opportunities than it is to encourage them.

MEASURING UNEMPLOYMENT

One of the larger measures used to indicate how well the U. S.

economy is doing has been to measure the numbers of people who are unemployed. It seemed a fairly good way to tell how many people had employment and a good measure of consumer spending, attitudes and other behaviors. In 2013, we heard more and more about a new measurement as we discussed the unemployment rate. As people began to ask questions regarding the questionable conclusions being made based on unemployment rates – and some rates that seemed out of sync with reality, the government began to mention the workforce participation rate. While the government hd been using that measure for some time, it was now being used to explain the apparent mismatch of reality with the unemployment numbers. From the bean counters running The United States Government, we got this explanation: "You see, some people have simply given up on finding a job. We can't really count them as unemployed if they are not looking, can we?" Balderdash. This is simply more proof of why larger government will not work. You can't trust them. Even if you entrust government to "help", they will find some way to stretch the truth. In the case of unemployment, it is all a shell game. Always has been, and always will be.

What is a good measure of unemployment? Are you employed? Is your neighbor employed? That is a good measure. The government doesn't call it what it is, the government calls it what they want you to think it is. Pure and simple.

UNEMPLOYMENT INSURANCE

Unemployment and the insurance that goes with it have been another very large social experiment by the United States government. Once in place, the insurance simply moves the standard of living around and delays any sort of response or feeling of urgency surrounding the obtaining of the unemployed person's next position. Moreover, the manipulation of the fund - which is, technically, insurance - causes some to feel as if the proceeds of the unemployment insurance are a part of the enormous entitlement component of government. In that case, many begin to feel, as some do with Social Security that the government "owes" them the tiny stipend that is unemployment insurance.

Sometimes the recipients are reticent to comply with requirements to receive the funds because they do not understand the purpose of the program and the designed temporary nature of the benefits paid.

It is also a counterproductive program. It fails to make use of a very large segment of society by "parking" them in a holding pattern waiting for their next assignment. Without clarification that the benefit is insurance, not an entitlement, the person may not be using the proceeds in the most effective way possible. Unlike the other social programs (welfare, food stamps, etc) which are taxpayer funded, the unemployment insurance similar to your automobile or personal accident insurance.

There are many ways to make the program more successful. As a part of a much larger "workfare" program, unemployment insurance could also become an opportunity for skilled or unskilled workers to gain new skills, or enhance the skills they already have. I am a member of The Church of Jesus Christ of Latter Day Saints. Our church has a great approach to administer programs designed to aid people in gaining or re-gaining full employment. These programs begin with a full assessment of the person's employability. The unemployed attend an all day seminar on how to secure employment. Temporal needs are assessed and addressed. Finally, those receiving assistance are given opportunities to perform work for those who need service, or to perform work from which they may learn or hone their skills. Certainly, the idea that when unemployed, a person's fulltime job is to become re-employed is an idea worth focusing on during periods of unemployment. Full consideration of a person's marketability, skill set, and needs is a good goal during these periods of unemployment.

In this plan, the goal is to become more fully employed and to build in lifestyle changes that ensure a more sustainable lifestyle. This includes a plan for fiscal solvency and for more conservative economics on a home budget. The fundamental safety net that comes from conservative living makes more sense and provides more security.

Unfortunately, some in government are being lobbied by those predators that prey on people with insufficient life skills. Pay day loans, check advances, bank fees and other predatory practices are for profit and depend on a certain part of the society to provide those customers. The teaching of sound fiscal behavior helps those who choose to adhere to the principles breaks a pattern of behavior that may have had the person and their family imprisoned by their own poor choices.

On the other side of the equation, beneficiaries of the program could provide needed training and mentoring for others as a segment of the job market adjusts to ever-changing trends in local markets. As unions have been demonized, we have lost an important aspect of skill creation. The unions provided internship and other opportunities for people to learn a trade. If we took those who are on unemployment, maintained them while unemployed and allowed them to teach others while drawing the unemployment, the labor market would benefit. But if commoditization in the labor market is the true goal of government, it is reasonable that government would not want to put people to work while drawing unemployment.

During my last period of unemployment, where I was told by a dear friend who taught the class at my church - "Until you go back to work, getting another job IS your job!"

How much better could we administer the government unemployment program? Much better. For anyone who has ever filed for and received unemployment insurance, it is not an active process. The person receiving the stipend is reduced to filling out a number of forms, checking a certain number of boxes, possibly attending a class or two, and then left to their own devices in obtaining their next position.

In its current form, unemployment insurance encourages the near term unemployed to wait for a job to come to them. It also encourages those for whom benefits have run out to drop below the radar, to become part of the underground employment market, or to simply give up hope of ever becoming employed again. Consequently, the official "unemployment rate" is skewed as the measure is altered by those who no longer choose to participate. Today, while the published unemployment rate is still publicly released, very few believe this number has any meaning as an indicator of workforce engagement. Certainly, another number is being released which may be a better indicator of the commoditization of workers. The workforce participation rate measures those who no longer participate in the job market. When considering the unemployment rate moves by less than one percent, one could argue the market looks pretty good. But when one considers a participation rate that moves ever higher, one could argue the unemployment rate is not the correct indicator of workforce performance.

I believe it is safe to say that in general, government programs don't work because they are often poorly designed, poorly implemented, poorly executed, and have no way to measure their effectiveness. In those cases where they may be measured for effectiveness, the results are often misinterpreted to the benefit of the program. Remembering that the US government has been proved to manipulate its citizens, it should be no surprise that unemployment insurance has not been the most effective way to administer this relief, and with the commoditization of the labor market it may actually make things worse as the commoditized get better at remaining employed in the commoditized space to the possible exclusion of the chronically unemployed.

I use unemployment insurance as an illustration only. Replace the conversation using social security, public education, food stamps, welfare or the myriad of other government programs, and collectively they make a great case for getting government out of those businesses. Unfortunately, so much of the U. S. is now composed of large segments dependent on government subsidies, it is almost impossible to reverse course.

This is just one more example of why we are experiencing a dysfunctional government. That dysfunction may have spread to the job market as a result, aiding in the creation of the commoditized worker. In my book "Return US to Liberty" you will see ideas about how to fix this broken system. Later in this book, we will discuss the future of labor in this country.

DISASSEMBLING THE AMERICAN INDUSTRIAL COMPLEX

Is it possible we have allowed ourselves to deliberately disassemble the American industrial complex? Certainly much of the industrialized America we once needed has now been dismantled; apparently on purpose. Arguably, some of that is due to our use of different or better technologies for manufacturing, production of items using different materials and the efficiency coming from improvements in processes.

What other indicators/motivators are there for this massive change

in America?
Here again is another reason why you have to take time to pay attention to politics. As a citizen of the United States, you would think that your representatives would be watching out for you and for your family. You might think the politicians would be looking at the government's impact on your future and the future of the country. But you don't have the power that other countries, their governments, global financiers, or even American corporations have to get your representatives' attention. Lobbyists for special interests get far more attention than the "working man". Particularly since the unionized work force has been disparaged and loathed since Ronald Reagan decertified The Professional Air Traffic Controllers Organization (PATCO) in 1981, the union lobby no longer carries the weight it once did when competing for the attention of politicians. Consequently, the politicians see no reason to take care of the working class, other than to provide additional social programs.
This has been one of the issues with the downturn in union membership. One could argue the unions were the lobbyists for the American workforce on any number of subjects, jobs, supporting families, pay equity and others.
America has been a leader in the world in innovation, mass production and industrialization. Many of the production methods of the world originated in the United States. A large percentage of engineers in the world obtain their education in American schools. So why is it that America seems to no longer be the world leader in

innovation and the production of goods and services?
By now, you know what this book will say. I hope you have at least taken into account the evidence of the possibility that America is being manipulated into second or third rate status in the world.
Big government, combined with corporatism, has self interest at heart in almost everything they do. This means protection of United States interests often comes as a secondary effort to the lobbyists and the companies they represent. Corporatism knows no boundaries. Rather than being divided along political philosophy or social lines, corporatism chooses a more elitist and economically segregated method of division, allowing money to decide what is in their best interest.
Commoditization has also come as a result of the reduction of almost everything else in America to the production of profit, the ultimate product. The corruption of free markets has caused corporations to lose sight of the need to protect the balance of free markets and capitalism. What is left is a sort of mafia rule open only to members of "the club". Democrat or Republican, Liberal or Conservative, choosing which lobbyist really does not matter much. In this regard, the difference between Republican or Democrat, Conservative or Liberal is likely not to play a large part in the decisions of those determining the long term standing of Americans and their labor market. One need only look at how the Democrat Party has turned its back on the union and labor movements in the United States, or how quickly almost all United

States Senators and Congressmen have left their positions more wealthy than when they arrived. Most politicians seem to be for sale to the highest bidder. In those transactions the working class is largely absent because they appear not to have been invited to the negotiations.

In addition, American industry was one of its strongest selling points for many years. Our ability to manufacture a wide array of products, including airplanes, cars and roads kept us safe from those who would do us harm. Consider during World War II when the country (and the world) needed to defend itself from genuine international threats. Conversion of America's industry base to support the war effort was a relatively simple matter.

As we dismantle those systems, one could argue we are dismantling our national defense. Does anyone see that? If they do, why are they not opposing it? It is not difficult to come to the conclusion that this might be treasonous behavior. Why would we want to expose the nation to the possibility that a component necessary for the defense of our nation would be produced by a country that might choose not to sell it to us, or could not get it here, if and when needed to defend our country? In this regard, commoditization weakens the country.

Entertain, for a moment, the thought that foreign governments want to defeat America, or at least weaken the country and its premier standing in the world. Rather than start an overt war by conventional means, isn't it possible that those governments would simply invade the United States by peaceful means and disassemble it from within? Disassembling the American industrial complex could be a sign of intention to remove the US from power and bring it down through economic means. Combined with recent moves towards internationalization and the massive US debt, there is plenty of evidence of subversives "both foreign and domestic" acting with intent to do harm to the United States. In that case, commoditization fits the plan….

Go to Google and type in Columbia University. Then search for articles on Marxism. There you will find multiple discussions on how to dismantle the capitalist system, virtually all of them propose it be done from within. Combined with the current trillions of dollars the United States owes in debt, this certainly seems more than plausible.

DEEP POCKET INFLUENCE

In 2013, Bill Gates could be found partnering with China, India and other foreign countries for innovation in science and technology. One might say it is almost treasonous that a man who made his fortune on a product that originated in the United States would co-opt with a foreign country for the next wave of innovation. One might also say that it makes sense that Mr. Gates would work to spread free enterprise to other countries. But it is hard to see the positives in that option given the taking advantage that comes from the oppressive labor policies of those countries. A man with Bill Gates' innovative mind (and deep pockets) could hardly be expected to allow government over-regulation to keep him from encouraging that innovation. One has to believe there is room for reason and moderation in these regulatory actions. It appears Mr. Gates is aware of the cost of over-regulation and has chosen to simply go elsewhere to avoid the associated costs.

This is not to say the deep pocketed financiers are completely wrong in taking their money outside the U.S. When analyzing their choices it is easy to see why an investor would choose to spend his money elsewhere. Given the inherent risk in investing combined with high taxes and regulation, the combined risk is too high.

EXPORTING JOBS?

After NAFTA, we watched many American manufacturing jobs go to Mexico, Canada, Japan, India, Taiwan and multiple other locations throughout the globe. The jobs that left were arguably the very core of the American economy. When GM and other auto manufacturers began building feeder plants in Mexico and elsewhere, there can be no doubt that at least part of their motivation was to escape the oppressive tax and regulatory structure they found in the United States. While these costs were onerous, the reduced cost of the foreign offshore work forces was a large influencer as well.

During that same period, we watched technical support and help desk jobs move "offshore", primarily to India, taking that labor segment out of the country as well.

Despite the complaints of most of those who experienced the language and cultural barriers of offshore support, the financial incentives to move those sectors offshore were too great. The ability to escape onerous regulation of labor markets, including the U. S. government imposed legislation for health care, caused many companies to force on their customers the poor customer service of offshore companies.

There are plenty of cases for good regulation. Certainly, as a society we do not want to be exposed to asbestos in our homes or workplace, dangerous chemicals in our water, or carbon and other chemicals in our air. We do not want to go to work in an unsafe environment, be forced to work long hours, or have our children working in "sweat shops". But there needs to be some reason in the regulation that protects us. When those regulations prove to be the root cause of a loss of jobs, one should consider their impact on the commoditization of the American workforce. Even in the case of "good" regulation, a high moral and ethical standard combined with free enterprise would have just as much impact when the customer decides not to purchase the goods causing the undesirable behavior.

Using regulation, an over reaching government has stifled innovation. This regulation has helped to create the commoditization we now see in our labor market. As a contract employee, the commoditized worker is isolated from most of the over-regulation due to their detachment from the work force. Many processes have been diminished. Anything containing questionable chemicals and other process related injury have simply moved to a different place on the planet.

EDUCATION

There can be no question that education has played a role in the success of the United States. As the country moved from an agricultural economy to an industrial economy, and as the population increased, the need for a "formal" education increased. In the late 1800's and early 1900's, there were many colleges and universities in the United States. There were also many trade schools. In some cases, workers learned their talents as they did their jobs each day. Apprenticeship, internship and other programs allowed workers to become tradesmen by giving the worker actual experience in their trade.

After the production line came into existence, unions assumed some of the role of training, providing internships and other methods for creating tradesmen in specialized tasks. Each of these entities provided their own types and versions of education and training, with career paths tied to success in the early days of the internship programs.

This also required an enormous amount of knowledge and skill on the part of the workforce. People depended on these options in order to secure their career, provide their livelihood and survive.

Prior to 1960, physicians, lawyers, engineers, accountants, teachers and others all went to a college or university, but the majority of the American workforce received education largely through experience. Combined with the universal training many received in the US military, there was a mindset of a "can-do" attitude as the foundation of many ideas.

An occasional farmer might have gone to college as the agriculture field realized they needed skilled workers with advanced knowledge of the sciences of agriculture and horticulture. Veterinarians were crucial to the care of livestock, horses and other farm animals, requiring advanced education in that specialization as well. Like physicians, this specialty took years of training. But the work of farming depended on the tradesmen – farmers who knew how to farm.

With the long standing tradition of employment of blacksmith, farmer, carpenter, there were a number of other trades developing in the early 1900's. As newer and more advanced skills were needed, the trades had apprenticeship programs for developing talents and providing knowledge. When unions came into being, they quite naturally grabbed on to the apprenticeship programs, expanding them to ensure the union members were sufficiently trained and educated in their respective trades. Movement from one level to the next as a union member meant additional pay, benefits and responsibility in a natural progression that took time and patience. Quite possibly, the patience required to progress may have also contributed to the demise of the union as workers demanded to be deemed a master at their trade without actually doing the work needed to earn them the "master" designation. To that end, education institutions offered an apparent "fast track" to a higher level. In some cases that was true. In others, it was not.

With the advent of the GI Bill in 1944, over 4 million Americans gained access to education at the college level. In the mid 1960's, there was the government's "Great Society" program. With it came the Higher Education Act of 1965. While the federal government had toyed with financing of college tuition since 1958, this act put the federal government firmly in the business of tuition assistance. Arguably, this was the beginning of what I refer to as "retail education".

From that point, the federal government spent large amounts of time and money on a variety of programs designed to encourage college attendance and provide financing for higher education opportunities. The base of these was originally the Perkins Loan and the Pell Grant. Combined with the VA program, a large number of people were injected into the work force after having taken time to gain skills or knowledge necessary to their chosen trade. Arguably, skill became secondary to knowledge, and both of them became commodities.

Today, the pursuit of an advanced education has created entire industries. From the companies that provide the financing, to companies that provide specialized training and certifications to junior colleges and beyond, each of these has a financial incentive for advocating for a higher education. However, I always refer back to my dad's comment – "If you want to make a living, be a plumber". Who says everyone needs a degree in order to make a living? Where are the service trades such as mechanic, carpenter, plumber and others? Does a plumber need a degree?

STUDENT LOANS

This year, outstanding student loan balances reached an all-time high of $1.12 trillion – an increase of $124 billion since last year, according to the New York Federal Reserve. Nearly 11 percent of aggregate student loan debt was at least 90 days delinquent or in default, as Politico reported last week

College graduates now leave school with an average of $26,500 in student loan debt – $4,600 more than the average student graduated with in 2001. Federal subsidies now account for 71 percent of all student aid. According to the College Board, over the past 10 years, the number of students borrowing through federal student loans increased by 69 percent.

Increases in debt have been driven by increases in college costs. In the last 30 years, inflation-adjusted tuition and fees at private colleges increased by 153 percent. Tuition and fees at public universities for in-state students increased 231 percent.

College costs have risen more than health care costs—by some estimates, twice as much—and faster than increases in the price of food. State-level spending has increased 88 percent since 1999.

Increases in tuition and fees over the past 30 years suggest that growth in federal subsidies such as loans and grants has done little to mitigate the college cost problem. And all of this spending and debt is not producing adequate outcomes:

• The 6-year college graduation rate stands at 59 percent. Just 41 percent of undergraduates complete college within 4 years.

• According to the Center for College Affordability and Productivity, 48 percent of working college graduates held jobs that did not require a college degree in 2010. Thirty-seven percent were in jobs that only required a high school diploma.[23]

(Burke, 2014)

"PUBLIC" EDUCATION

The creation of public education was the beginning of a big government push into that arena. In concert with unions in the beginning the work of assimilating students into public education continued. This is also where the existence of capitalism presented a conflict of interest of sorts, one that exists in modern times as well. During this entire period, the United States found itself involved in "retail education". The taxpayer would pay for education. Then, for a fee, the taxpayer would get some "free" education. But just like most things coming from the government, what the taxpayer received for their investment was not what it appeared to be.

Education was commoditized by the U. S. government when it began controlling the content of what students would receive. Once the content was under control and measurable, commoditization was complete.

Education is such a strong influence in commoditization that it gets it's own section in the book. But remember, the United States

---

[23] http://dailysignal.com/2014/08/19/average-student-loan-debt-just-keeps-rising/?utm_source=facebook&utm_medium=social

government has been the strongest influencer in education, continually expanding into that arena. Arguably, the US government has failed in the effort to educate the citizens. Certainly, the assimilation and indoctrination that occur in public education have worked to the detriment of the nation and certainly continued the commoditization of the American worker.

In 2014, the United States government is engaged in a program ominously titled “Common Core”. While some in federal government remind us that Common Core is a state initiative, others have shown it to be a very large federal initiative. As with many government programs, it was rolled out rapidly and without the close scrutiny a program of this magnitude demands.

It appears Common Core has other goals as well. In math questions, new and different social concepts become the “new normal”. Many math problems are that were once solved by simple methods become complex. Historical facts are changed. Given the history of government in instituting social change, it has become evident Common Core is as much, if not more, about indoctrination to government defined normal as about the education of our youth.

ANTI-UNION GOVERNMENT

Toward the end of the 1980’s, the U. S. government decided the labor unions were the country's enemy. Starting with the PATCO decertification, an open opposition to unions grew into a movement of sorts. With questions about corruption, inefficiency, costly labor and, ultimately, control of privately owned businesses, government led the way in the fight against unions. While the Democrat Party was once the party of labor, they began not to get involved in advocating for labor or labor unions.

In 2014, Volkswagen manufacturing in Chattanooga Tennessee had a vote to determine unionization of their newly created manufacturing facility. Volkswagen remained neutral on the idea, although they were a party to the request filed with NLRB to have the union vote. Their position was that all of their other manufacturing facilities were unionized and that their relationship with labor was solid enough to withstand unionization.

On the other side of the argument, government and politicians got involved. Governor Bill Haslam said if the workers voted for the union representation, parts vendors would not come to Tennessee. [24]The State House threatened to revoke three hundred million dollars in tax breaks for Volkswagen if the union initiative passed. And U. S. Senator Bob Corker started a rumor that a second line of cars would not be built there if the union was voted in. Volkswagen quickly denied those rumors, but the damage was appeared to be done. (The second car line was ultimately brought to Volkswagen.)[25]

The vote was 712 – 626. Not the crushing defeat some media

---

[24] http://www.nashvillescene.com/pitw/archives/2014/04/01/did-bill-haslam-lie-about-pressuring-vw-over-unions

[25] http://www.huffingtonpost.com/2014/02/18/bob-corker-volkswagen-uaw-vote_n_4810757.html

outlets alluded to, but a defeat nonetheless. The UAW rapidly filed an appeal based on illegal government interference. That appeal was suddenly dropped when the UAW and Volkswagen came to an agreement for representation of workers in a non-binding relationship that continues to be refined.

What the unions had been doing in providing internships and other training opportunities in the trades was replaced by yet another government program, albeit a privately run program. Offering up massive student loans, the government encouraged almost everyone to go to college and incur debt if they had to in order to "get an education" or “earn a degree”.

The schools and other educational institutions were happy to provide these new training programs, for a profit. The banks and the government were happy to get into the financing of education where there were obviously millions, if not billions, of dollars to be made. The student loan program turned into a cash cow - but for whom? According to the latest projections from the CBO, the federal government will earn about $127 billion over the next ten years from its recently acquired role as the direct provider of most student loans.[26]

There are currently more than four hundred seventy thousand people in default on their student loans. The White House puts the

---

[26] http://www.forbes.com/sites/jeffreydorfman/2014/04/19/student-loan-profits-show-government-should-get-out-of-student-loan-business/

rate for 2011 at ten percent.[27] Default rates for 2012 were as high as thirteen percent. Many of them are in default because they were unable to get employment in the fields they chose. In some cases the very existence of student loans flooded industries with more talent than they needed. In my case, technology simply did away with the career for which I had borrowed money. The "glass cockpit", technology that replaced the analog instruments and guidance and control systems in most aircraft, eliminated my job in less than a ten year time span.

In the case of an attempt by the student to default, there is very little hope for the student.[28] Legislators, often under the influence of powerful lobbyists, engineered the treatment of defaulted student loans in the favor of the lender. There are deferment and other programs with usurious interest rates and penalties as high as 20%. Legislators exempted student loan debt from bankruptcy. The bankruptcy court cannot protect a debtor. The penalties for non-payment of a student loan are as usurious as any predatory lending program. The scarcity of jobs make the likelihood a person will repay the loan very slim if the person is unable to find work.

In all of this effort toward education and adoption of retail education, what occurred? We managed to create a retail education industry that does a poor job of giving people real skills, but a great job of giving the impression someone is qualified for the

---

[27] http://www2.ed.gov/offices/OSFAP/defaultmanagement/cdr2yr.html

[28] http://www.debt.org/students/bankruptcy/

work they want to do. Commoditized education is for sale to the commoditized person who uses commoditized financing to pay for it. All of this is geared towards massive profits for banks, other financial institutions and schools. The result is massive, crippling debt for students and other borrowers.

At the end of the day, many consider the education has simply been average. Nothing outstanding or earth shattering, just average. Does everyone need a college degree? Does everyone need an advanced education? Is the process of government education creating tradesmen, artisans and innovative thinkers capable of creating and maintaining new innovations that are being introduced? I propose the commoditization of labor was brought on partially through the commoditization of finance and the conversion of education to a retail delivery model.

CREDIT

By now, you realize that credit is not your friend. Having that new house, or new car, or new whatever - without owning it - has become a weight around your neck. Likewise, the government's influence to your getting credit has contributed to the changes that impact your ability to get work. It has also become another source of stress as you struggle to pay those mountainous student loans and other credit items, some of which you could and should do without, but choose badly to take the offer. Really, how does a sophomore in college get a two thousand dollar credit card?

I am sure you have been astonished at the offers of credit that came to you or your children as they entered college. They start early with the financing of education, (financing that includes living expenses). By the time the financing is factored in, the cost of rent and food covered by the student loans will be out of sight. There is also the opportunity to add to that mountainous debt with consumer credit. Unmanaged and without good decisions, that credit becomes like an anchor around the student's neck.

The use of credit has masked the concept that some things are worth waiting and saving for. Instant gratification makes it appear that the life of an American, which is already a life of abundance, is so abundant that there is nothing that can keep us from enjoying everything immediately. This concept has been pervasive as society and the government continues to add up debt regardless of the ability to pay that debt back. In many cases, educational institutions do not typically teach about debt management because sales have become more important than education for many of these institutions.

CAUSES OF CREDIT

Part of this free flow of credit stems from the fact that the government is so heavily indebted. In 2014, the United States Government was in debt for 17.6 Trillion dollars, much of that to foreign entities.

Other causes included the role credit has in providing access to other commodities for which Americans have typically saved. Many large purchase items come with financing from companies who have a relationship with the commodity vendor simply because without financing, people would keep whatever they have.

IMPACT OF GOVERNMENT ECONOMIC POLICY

Another reason for the debt is the existence of the Federal Reserve. The Federal Reserve, which has essentially become the nationalized bank President Andrew Jackson fought against, prints money at will, manipulating the money in the country and by extension manipulating the price of all the things money can buy. Since the mid 1970's when President Nixon took the US economy off the gold standard, the Fed has attempted to monetize credit markets, including bonds and securities. The financial impact of this type of government behavior is that it encourages less than frugal behavior on the part of people in the country.

INTERNATIONAL TRADE

Beginning in the mid-1980s, American manufacturers began reaching outside American borders for sales opportunities. Notice I said sales, not manufacturing. It is quite natural for a sales person to want to continually grow their market. Unfortunately, this is not as simple as it looks. Selling finished products is one thing, but selling raw materials or commoditized products is quite another. Once the U.S. manufacturers exposed the breadth of their coverage in multiple products, foreign manufacturers began the process of injecting their costs into the U. S. market.

The United States is somewhat unique in the way markets appear. The system of ownership in a free society is quite different from the system of ownership in a country where the citizens are controlled by the government.

When controlled by government, who gets what is determined by how they behave rather than how hard they work. If they get a home, a car, a TV or many other items depends almost entirely on their alignment with, or opposition to, the prevailing government in the country in which they live, as well as their compliance with government imposed rules.

It is possible the move toward international trade (access to foreign markets) began the commoditization of the American workforce. In negotiating the right to sell American goods to other countries, those countries often insisted the manufacturing and distributing be brought to their own countries. Reasonable enough. But that skews the dynamic of the process. The parameters around international sales and manufacturing are vastly different. Add to that the opportunity to make more money on the part of American companies (because of "cheap" labor subsidized by American and foreign governments), and to some it might have appeared to be a completely winning proposition for all involved. Except for the working class American, that is likely to have been the case.

When American companies go to foreign countries to sell and manufacture their products, the rules of that country begin to influence the company and its operations. What is considered unethical in the United States might not seem unethical in a foreign country. Using pre-teen labor, sweat shops, unsafe buildings, and unethical business deals all seem normal in some markets. When American products try to compete in those spaces, it is simply not possible.

Certainly, the language barrier, even when the international company appears to speak some English and seems to understand it well, presents unusual problems. It is one thing to hear and converse in English when it is not your native tongue. It is quite another to understand the conversation. While some are convinced this is not an issue, many of my peers agree with me when I say we are having a conversation, but we do not understand one another.

Cultural and ethical business practices are different. The tendency to deceive and to present less than factual statements is viewed as normal business practice in some countries. To the contrary, U. S companies generally view deception as unacceptable.

You ask what the options are in that case? The role of the United States is to raise the standards of the world. Setting a higher standard should be the goal of our efforts in international markets. Higher standards should be one of the items we export. For years in the early 1900s, labor in the United States went through a metamorphosis – and set a standard for labor practices across the world. When mine workers were dying in mine accidents, companies improved the working conditions. When children were found working in sweat shops, the United States stopped the process. Even when workers traded their time for money, Americans determined that time away from their families was worth at least one and one half times as much as the regular hours spent away from their families.

In many cases, the world's labor standards were measured against the higher standards of U. S. workers. These improvements in standards were the standard to which people across the world looked for guidance and for proof of what method worked.

CURRENCY MANIPULATION

Early in America's history, President Andrew Jackson fought hard for the United States to not have a national bank. His reasons were quite clear. He and others felt this entry of the U. S. government into the financial system was a violation of Constitutional principles.

Today, we have the Federal Reserve. The Federal Reserve has the ability to manipulate and otherwise alter the value of United States currency. With no basis in a hard currency (President Nixon took the U. S. off of the gold standard, there is no fixed value of the American dollar. It is worth whatever the government says it is worth. Through the printing of additional baseless currency, the Fed simply creates more money whenever it needs it.

ANTI-UNION BEHAVIOR

We will refer to anti-union behavior a few times in this book. One could see this entire effort to demonize unions was an organized plan on the part of big business, big banks and many others to remove unions, while also giving the American worker something to focus on besides the fact that they were being commoditized. The United States government became subject to the influence of big money, big banks and foreign governments through their close relations as internationalization had been introduced through the

UN's desire to have a One World Order or New World Order (Agenda 21). It is logical, then, that the government's need for (or tolerance of) unions became diminished over time. Once that switch had occurred, the clock was ticking on America's union movement – and on the American middle class. The role of unions would never be the same. Workforce commoditization inevitably had to follow.

At some point, after the surrender of the Democrat advocates of union labor, the government began caving in to anti-union efforts by lobbyists from big business, big money and the lobbyists that control the politicians. The government began actively participating in the systematic dismantling of the unions. You might ask why? The logical answer is that American unions had been protecting American jobs for their entire history. The people involved realized the only way they could successfully export jobs from America was to develop and cultivate an anti-union movement in the United States.

In the 1980s, the unions handed the anti-union movement the key to their own demise. Picking a fight with Ronald Reagan, PATCO (The Air Traffic Controllers Union) threatened a walkout. Reagan warned the union if they did not return to work he would simply replace them all and de-certify the union. The stage was set. In the end, the test case for minimizing unions was won when President Reagan replaced all the air traffic controllers and conquered their union. It was a very pivotal event and the unions did it to themselves.

The anti-union movement was a red herring, a ruse, in the battle to commoditize American labor. Whether unions drove companies into bankruptcy and out of existence; whether the relatively recent demise of Detroit is caused by bad politics, unions, or something else is a debate that will last forever. One could argue that unions did make unreasonable demands (and they often did). But one could just as easily argue that bad managers and executives allowed that to happen. In that argument, the managers and executives had a balancing act; a fiduciary responsibility to the company, retention of appropriate talent, and maintenance of market share. I propose the difference between those companies that failed and those that succeeded was not entirely union influence. Some of that was poor management of the union influence.

THE FORD ARGUMENT

Consider for a moment the argument that unions destroyed the automotive industry in the United States. With their demands for ever higher wages, benefits, security and other issues, they simply drove the U. S. producers out of the business. Chrysler and GM were bankrupt and had to take the U. S. Government stimulus in order to survive. The U. S. government purchased a part of the companies to keep them from going bankrupt.

On the other hand, Ford Motor Company, while dealing with the same union, flourished. With plenty of cash in the bank, solid labor relations and a thriving market share, Ford continued to be a solvent multi-national auto producer.

What was the difference? Leave unions out of the conversation for a second. Could it be that a wiser management structure kept Ford alive? Could it be those managers were more frugal, provided a more solid disaster plan? Could it also be the Ford managers simply managed the union better as well? If your answer is yes, then consider that – whether the union caused GM to fail or not, GM management ultimately was the primary cause of the failure either way.

I know this once again sounds like a conspiracy theory. I wish it did not. I am anxious to hear a more reasoned explanation for the series of anti union events as a whole. When looking at the entire picture, it seems fairly obvious that the giant social experiment called the United States of America contains a sinister manipulation of the lives of all Americans. The United States government has shown a blatant disregard for its citizen's liberties for a very long time. Becoming the enemy of the working class was a sign that even the government was happy to demonize the hard working citizens who made the country the leader it had become. Now, those hard working citizens would pay the price by becoming commoditized.

It is unquestionable that as the United States government has grown. It has had its hands in any number of issues causing commoditization. How could we have prevented this from happening? How do we hold government accountable? Is it possible to reverse the commoditization process?

It is clear that the influence of each segment covered in this book has been geared toward influencing the government to make decisions that benefit that entity. After this review, a person should be able to make up their mind about whether big government has been successful in protecting the interests of the country, or whether big government has been ineffective at those protections.

SUMMARY

Speaking about government in reference to commoditization of labor can lead us to many conclusions. The simple act of including government in this book goes to the basic argument of what role government(s) should play in a society such as the United States. It is difficult to imagine the United States without the integration of at least a federal government, but state governments should have their own approach as well. There are many things that government does that have tremendous theoretical positive impacts.

However, the role of government in general, and in American society specifically, has been to perform the following functions, none of which is authorized by the United States Constitution:

1) Tax
2) Create Law
3) Enforce Law
4) Redistribute and otherwise influence wealth
5) Regulate many things – commerce among them.
6) Educate (indoctrinate) the American public

We can argue about the impact of taxes and of regulation. Many have tried. But there are some incontrovertible facts:

1) Taxes play a serious role in all parts of American life. The damage done from taxes, especially when the government has a voracious appetite, can be seen throughout society.

2) The creation of law should not be up to the government. The creation of law should be left up to the citizens. The creation of laws by governments creates a conflict of interest. In our Constitutional Republic, the representative form of government allows for the will of the people by designating representatives who create law. Whether that system is corrupt is a point of debate. One could argue that the more laws that are created, the less freedom our society will enjoy. Making something illegal will not necessarily stop it from happening and will certainly give more power to the government run police state.

3) One could argue that enforcing laws is part of the Constitutional mandate to provide security and to provide for the general welfare of the citizenry. However, this only works in the purest sense. When governments create the laws without input from the citizens, then engage in enforcement of those laws, the tendency towards elitism, bribery, graft and selective enforcement is rampant.

4) Income redistribution has been at the center of the debate on the role of government. An exclusive condition of the United States, the middle class, has been one of the strengths of the economy of our country. One could argue the commoditization of the American work force occurred simultaneously with the virtual elimination of

the middle class.

5) Regulation of anything by the U. S. government very quickly turns into tyranny of sorts. On a small scale, the tyranny of oppression, compulsion and judgment have resulted in the commoditization of labor.

6) It is true that most education can be classified as some sort of assimilation and might even be indoctrination. When exercised over free thinking and behaving people, this can be good. But once again, when a government engages in education and controls the content, the tendency to use that assumed authority to manipulate the population for other evil goals is very popular.

Is the government evil? Certainly not. Is it misguided? I don't believe anyone would argue that corruption and bad behavior do not exist in any government in 2014. Is it possible this contributed to commoditization? Absolutely!

CONCLUSIONS

Government in the United States has gotten too big, too powerful, and too demanding. As it fed its appetite for money and power, the United States government, influenced by almost every special interest one can think of, allowed or caused the commoditization of a labor force that supported the American way of life for decades.

Chapter 5

Unions

Unions began in the United States in the late 1800's. With people like Samuel Gompers of The American Federation of Labor, (Otherwise known as the "AFL" part of the more familiar AFL-CIO), they began fighting for fair treatment in the form of safety, compensation and benefits.. Their original intent was to provide for the safety of the workplace in a time when much of the labor force faced severely physically demanding tasks. In addition, many laborers performed this physical work for long hours in dangerous circumstances, so unions began to be concerned with workplace safety as well. The rate of death in American workplaces was extremely high. For instance, from 1911 through 1997, approximately 103,000 miners died at work. During 1911–1915, an average of 3329 mining-related deaths occurred per year among approximately 1 million miners employed annually, with an average annual fatality rate of 329 per 100,000 miners. During the century, the average annual number of workers (operators and contractors combined) in the mining industry has declined to approximately 356,000, and deaths have dropped approximately 37-fold, from 3329 to 89; injury fatality rates have decreased approximately 13-fold, to 25 per 100,000 during 1996–1997.[29] Unions became a very large and commanding force in the U. S. Their early role was to be the advocate for trades, manufacturing and other workers who served their industries in America, many which were growing rapidly. Unionized workers leveraged their power to negotiate against long work hours and unsafe conditions. Later, they would become involved in negotiations for benefits and other fairness issues.

For organized workers, there were struggles and trials with this model. Unions performed the work of "collective bargaining". Workers of common interest needed and were able to harness the energy that came from that effort. But this meant taking a stand, sometimes putting them in harm's way. Many union members lost wages, their jobs, and even their lives in the fight for workers' rights.

In the days of Samuel Gompers, many people, including children as young as 10 years of age, worked in deplorable conditions, for very long hours, under oppressive circumstances. More familiar would be the plight of the coal miners, many of whom died on a regular basis as they toiled underground bringing coal to the surface.

Truckers and auto workers organized labor and fought battles for their wages, safety and benefits as well. History is full of stories of the struggles of labor against industry throughout the early 1900's.

[29] http://www.cdc.gov/mmwr/pdf/wk/mm4822.pdf

Henry Ford was famous as an advocate for automation in the form of the assembly line. He was also famous for his advocacy of a "living wage" for those working in his assembly plants.
During the labor strikes of the late 19th and early 20th centuries, businessmen hired the Pinkerton Agency to infiltrate unions, supply guards, keep strikers and suspected unionists out of factories, as well as recruiting goon squads to intimidate workers. The Ford Motor Company engaged in a battle to lock workers out. At one point, battle between Pinkerton agents and striking workers led to the deaths of seven Pinkerton agents and nine steelworkers.[30]
This country enjoys a rich history of innovative and productive labor. From the beginning of the industrial revolution, American workers met the challenge of production work, manual labor and truck driving. They also met the need for skilled labor, carpentry, steel working, and welding. No matter the national priority, American workers filled the need very well, delivering some of the most amazing and challenging projects on time and within budget. In many cases, the companies which employed the union worker were at least neutral on the top three worker priorities: wages, benefits, and safety. Originally, skilled labor was taken for granted. Much of the improvement to the workplace in the early 1900's came as a result of the union movement. Unions very systematically organized workers who were putting in very long periods of work, often with no breaks, and under severe work

[30] http://en.wikipedia.org/wiki/Pinkerton_(detective_agency)

conditions, and in many cases without food and with sub-minimum wages that did not allow a person to support themselves, much less a family. Accident and mortality rates were high, extremely high in some professions. There were company stores providing basic necessities at exorbitant prices on credit.

The popular song' "sixteen tons" lyrics hinted at the dangers of working in mines and the hard times of living in mining communities. And indeed, from the early 1900s through the 1940s, life in the coal mining communities all across the country was pretty grim. Mineworkers were frequently killed in mine accidents and most who worked in the mines developed "black lung" disease from years of breathing coal dust. Although mine conditions improved following the unionization of mine workers in the 1930s and subsequent mine safety laws, even in the mid-1950s when "Sixteen Tons" was at the top of the charts, mine accidents and deplorable conditions in mining communities were still found throughout the coal fields.

And as "Sixteen Tons" made plain in its lyrics, indebtedness to the company was also a problem in some coal communities, especially before labor reforms were adopted. Coal miners often became indebted to the "company store," also known as the general store in some locations. With no competition, the company could keep prices high for everyday items, and employees – especially those with families – often needed to pay in credit with tokens or scrip. A never-ending cycle of debt often resulted, meaning essentially that the workers were perpetually bound to the company. [31]

Unions came in and, using collective bargaining, organized the workers into units whose goal was to ensure each other's safety and to somewhat control the skills of the workers who were assigned to do the work. After all, in some cases, those employees had other employees' lives in their hands.

Unions also held elections and the good ones solicited the opinions of the rank and file union members. There were contract negotiations giving priority to the members' needs and wants, and providing feedback to the company as to the issues needing the most attention. Union representatives did what the rank and file told them to do most of the time.

At some point, union leaders began making the decisions and sending the priorities down to the membership. In that regard, there is validity to the argument that members were mindlessly following union leadership. Much like the U. S. government relationship with its citizens, at some point the voters became subjects to the governmental organization.

Unions were always concerned with what I call "The Big Three" – wages, benefits, and workplace safety. There were other issues in many cases, but the focus was always primarily on these three issues. At some point, unions added control to their list of desires; clearly a bad idea, this would ultimately be the issue that caused

[31] http://www.pophistorydig.com/?tag=sixteen-tons-song-history

the union′ s undoing as they allowed that power and control to override their mandate to be an advocate for labor.
American industry, the American worker and the unions joined together as they forged new trails in the American labor market. Their influence in bringing the U. S. to the top of the world in terms of labor, productivity and economic freedom was significant. If only they had not lost direction because of the other influencers in the U. S, as we will see below.

THE U. S. GOVERNMENT

Beginning in the 1980's, the public perception of unions in the U. S. began to change. Did unions go too far in their advocacy of the big three? In many cases, we could argue they did. In their incessant quest for wages, benefits, and safety, the control they exercised became the issue upon which unions would rely for their influence. How could this happen? How could unions grow so large? One could argue that only when the U. S. government got involved did unions gain true power. Once the government became the enforcement arm of the union movement, and once that government began more actively participating in the labor movement through the creation of OSHA, the Department of Labor and other government agencies, did companies have to pay more attention to the demands of the unions. If only unions had realized those were temporary gains, they might not have been so unreasonable in exerting the force that ultimately brought them down and caused labor to become a commodity.

THE WINDS OF CHANGE

At what point did the current negative impression about unions begin? People were tiring of unions in the mid 1980's. The PATCO (Air Traffic Controllers) battle with Ronald Reagan was a catalyst in the anti-union sentiment. In their never ending efforts for more power over the organized companies, unions picked a fight with a highly popular President of the United States – and lost. Ronald Reagan refused to negotiate with the union and gave the unions a deadline to get back to work. The unions refused. Ronald Reagan fired them all. And the American public largely supported him in that action.

This began a more overt period where being against unions was popular. The sentiment against workers making "too much" money was becoming popular. Even then, commoditization was underway. In these conversations, no one seemed to know who determined "too much" when it came to compensation, but many appeared to agree unions had crossed that line.

There was a sense of resentment toward unions. Rather than something to which to aspire, people began to speak openly of the unfairness of union jobs when compared with the rest of American society.

Also during this period, the discussion began about whether government workers should have the right to strike. Some went so far as to say government workers should <u>not</u> have the right to organize or have a right to collective bargaining at all. That discussion continues through 2014 as the largest segment of unions to survive the anti-union efforts in the U. S. has become "public service" unions such as the SEIU, NEA and other unions purported to serve the needs of government workers.

GOVERNMENT WORKERS

Should government workers be unionized? Since the 1980's, many have been added to the list of those beginning to discuss government employees and whether they should be unionized. In the area of public service, there is currently an argument that making a career of public service has been a detriment to the U. S. and to the individual states themselves. One could argue the government service arena should have more patriots in its service than employees.

Returning to the PATCO instance, a case could be made that PATCO members were "government workers". Ronald Reagan destroyed that union and permanently removed the unions from that job classification. Why then have so many other leaders failed in their efforts? In 2013, Governor Scott Walker of Wisconsin engaged in such a battle. He was successful, permanently weakening the public unions in his state. Others appear to be ready to try.

Yet, many other government workers continue to be engaged in collective bargaining. In the service sector, organized workers are thriving even as service sector jobs in the private sector continue to decline in numbers as well as in compensation.

PUBLIC EDUCATION WORKERS

Should educators in our public schools be allowed to engage in collective bargaining and other sectors of unionization? Education is arguably another profession where public service is at its core. I believe the current public education system has been corrupted by its affiliation with unions such as the National Education Association (NEA) and others. In this area, the appearance has been that educators have chosen union objectives over their profession, or the education of their students. Certainly, the battle for wages and benefits presents union members as less than professional as they seemingly choose wages and benefits over high quality education for their students.

One could argue that what public education is doing is more about indoctrination or assimilation than it is about teaching. We will have that discussion elsewhere in this book.

Certainly, when considering the relationship between a government with which unions negotiate for the big three, when that same government wants to exercise what some would believe to be unconstitutional authority with programs such as Common Core, one could conclude the relationship is a conflict of interest.

MINDLESS ZOMBIES

I once heard a person describe union members as "mindless zombies". What an unfair characterization of the tradesmen, laborers and professionals involved in the unionized workforce over the last several generations.

Have some union members become part of a collective that did the bidding of their union mindlessly? Certainly. Similar to how citizens have blindly followed their political leaders and parties, some members have, without much thought, followed direction and plans not in their personal best interest. So-called low information voters can exist not only in the political realm but in any publicly run organization.

From entry level, through apprentice, and on to the tradesmen and journeymen, union members understand the value in "collective bargaining" which is the foundation of the union movement. Collective bargaining theoretically ensures labor negotiations follow a strict set of rules so that the process produces good wages, benefits and safety to the “collective”.

Is that method of negotiation now gone? Hardly. It has simply been changed in this commoditized job market. Rather than "collective" bargaining, workers engage a recruiting company that negotiates thru individual employment packages.

Are these workers "mindless"? I think not. As labor in the U. S. was commoditized, at least in the case of production line workers, their focus had been quite constant. Produce item A in time period B. In many cases, produce large quantities of a particular item. Was it required to do that safely? Maybe. Was it required to do that economically? We certainly hope so. Was it important to do that and still raise a family? The goal of many, it was a popular thought to raise a family. But any of those things requires much more than a mindless approach.

In the case of the services line of work, the options were slightly different, but the result was much the same. Go fix item A or any particular designated item; get paid.

WHAT ELSE IS THERE?

In the earliest times of organized labor, unions played a large role in determining the work force rules in the U. S. Beginning with Samuel Gompers, moving through Henry Ford and the Pinkerton crew, and ending with Ronald Reagan's de-certification of PATCO in the 1980's, unions ruled many companies. There was much unrighteous behavior and mob tactics from a number of sources, including the mob or organized crime.

This is where we begin to see the unrealistic relationship between unions and companies. The adversarial nature of this relationship was evident and counterproductive to all parties. Whether that adversarial approach was deliberate on either party's part is a subject for discussion. But that relationship began early and was pervasive throughout the term of unions including those unions today. I am left to wonder if unions today will be deliberate in their contentious approach. If so, there is no hope. If the contention is out of frustration, fear, or even mutual respect, there may be some hope for organized labor in the future.

There was something else that unions missed out on. Theirs was a monolithic view of "What else is there"? Union leaders typically came from the rank and file members. When it came time for unions and the labor they represented to move toward a position aimed at the future of labor, unions failed. Unions and their members continued to only pay attention to three things: work conditions, wages, and benefits. What else is there? Indeed.

HUNTING SEASON

When I was in the Ironworker's Union, I noticed that many union members looked forward to a strike. I was intrigued to discover many members were hunters and would time their strike votes to coincide with hunting season. No lie!

So, what is there to negotiate when the big three have been satisfied? If wages, benefits and work conditions are agreeable, unions tend to lose significance and import. Except for little arguments about unfair treatment, or taking long breaks, or doing someone else's job, there is not much for the union to do.

From the worker's viewpoint, the big three were all for which the union had to fight. We, as members, depended on the union to negotiate for us.

This relationship caused a division between the company and its labor, the workforce without whom the company could not produce the product that produced the money to pay not only the workforce, but all the vendors, real estate, overhead, administrative staff, and corporate salaries and stock holders.

So what else is there? How about tying performance and production to increases and bonuses; even for the workers? Establishing a base hourly wage, then assigning premiums for the tasks based on their level of difficulty and their quality? This was an unheard of concept and met with significant resistance many times, even though the potential for better pay was significant. In hindsight, some sort of co-opting with the union would have produced better results. Union ownership of specific tasks would have given a longer term solution allowing both labor and management to focus on a common goal.

It is clear that some companies failed to properly focus on their goals. The goals of quality and profitability were addressed at a few companies which thrived along with their union membership. One need only look at Ford Motor Company to see the successes in labor and union relations that failed in other in other industry competitors; most notably General Motors. The argument that company leadership allowed the union to destroy the company cannot be dismissed when considering the fact that Ford Motor Company survived and even thrived even though they had to deal with the UAW.

This may be what caused American quality to decline somewhat in the mid 1980's. When I was working as a union worker, our entire focus was on "making production". As a consequence, on some days or nights, quality was largely absent. 100% quality was non-existent. We produced the widget as rapidly as we could with very little concern for the part that fell off the line, was not installed correctly, or was simply missing. So long as we had the proper counts, we were getting paid and getting bonuses for the higher output.

Companies have gotten smarter about the value of labor and have adopted much better processes. As a manager, I learned about retention, recruitment, fairness, diversity and many other things that determined our success. Most of the people I managed were paid well, worked in a good environment, were not treated poorly, knew exactly where I stood on issues, and understood I was their biggest advocate for fairness. I worked hard to include everyone on the team. As a result, I had a great team with which to work.

Unions in America may have outlived their usefulness as a part of a natural cycle. I don't think the "hate unions" movement was necessary. In fact, current union relations may still be one of the biggest distractions to honest and successful workforce engagement in some companies.

Many companies have learned the lesson and stopped their contentious behavior. Many workers have likewise learned they need to provide value to the company which employs them. As a commoditized workforce, most workers now need to be able to show the value of what they are paid to do. In the commoditized model, companies understand the value of tradesmen and simply negotiate in good faith. The difference? A commodity has almost no returning value to a company. If a commodity provides ongoing value, the relationship is solid and ongoing. If, however, either party is not getting what they want, the relationship is over.

BAD UNION MANAGERS

I have been a member of the Ironworkers, Steelworkers, and The International Association of Machinists and Aerospace Workers Union at various times in my career. Each of these organizations

had been active in negotiating wages, benefits and working conditions. They also were built in to the operations of such companies as Production Steel in Nashville TN, Murray Steel in Nashville, and Lockheed Aeronautical Systems in Marietta, Ga.
At Production Steel and Murray Steel, the union management style was one of opposition and contention. Universally, each of the union members was skilled in their respective trades. They had experience in a number of steel handling methods, all of which contributed heavily to the production operation of the facilities. Unfortunately, those same union people engaged directly with the company were openly resistant to just about every company initiative. Moreover, they seemed to revel in the contentious relationship.
A slitter operator rarely helped the crane operator. The bander did not unload steel. The hooker never helped the bander. (Yes - I was a hooker) The punch operator never unloaded the truck.
At Lockheed, we also had an extensive group of tradesmen. Additionally, we had a much larger operation that contained significant numbers of people who simply went to work each day and assembled parts. We were isolated from union management. There was a very structured program for dealing with each other for almost all aspects of the operation. I was issued a small bound notebook with about 150 pages in it. This was a complete copy of the entire union contract. I memorized that book and knew exactly what the rules were as a result.
In each situation, the union always appeared to share the same

motivation - get more. One might ask "more of what"? The answer was simple - once wages, benefits and safety were addressed, get whatever you can. Often, “it” was simply power.

What the union missed was the opportunity to use better management as a tool to bring their product (people with specialized skills) to their customer. Could better union managers have come up with a way to make the unionization of workers more compatible with American companies? I believe they could have. Rather than creating “rank and file” members, unions should have empowered the tradesman with the capacity to understand business operations and all the components of that trade. This would have allowed them to find ways to join with a company to work toward better operations. As partners on a team, they could continue the fight against taxes, government regulation and the shipping of American jobs overseas.

I now wonder why the union movement was structured as it was. Surely they realized that by asking for more of everything, even when there was no more to get, the effort would eventually result in their asking for more when there truly was no more to give. Better union managers would have seen the negative impact of the union and found ways to fix that relationship.

Union leaders today continue to take well trained, proven, skilled tradesmen and "promote" them as union stewards or other leaders within the movement. Those people sometimes become business agents and other union leaders. What talent do they have to negotiate or understand the company's position? How can they be strategists? They often cannot. At a minimum, the union should assess a person's capacity for the change in tasks, and train them for those management functions.

Union leaders should have recognized early their real gains would have been in tying worker pay to performance. Squeezing companies for a piece of the company and profits would have been a better mechanism than simply going for the cash. Solid managers (for the union) would have recognized and cultivated ways to leverage this. Even today, unions continue their contentious approach to labor relations. Companies, and employees represented by unions, are doubtful this tactic has value any more. What is left for the unions are the government and education sectors. What a disservice to have government and education workers view their labor relations as opportunities for opposition.

BAD COMPANY MANAGERS

On the company's side, managers felt they were stuck with the unions. They sometimes got so distracted in the adversarial role; they failed to manage the company as well as they could have. I personally watched many times as a manager did something, often to the detriment of the team, just to show power over the union. The Hostess Company ceased production of Twinkies in early 2013 as a result of the continued insistence of unions to stick with legacy approaches, such as striking, shutdowns, and continued demand for high wages. Hostess simply shut down operations and walked away. The company purchasing the plant wanted to resume operations with non-union workers and there was very little surprise when that happened. This was simply another step in the path toward commoditization of American workers.

Companies developed a method of building pay and benefits into negotiations. This was the easy way out for them, sticking to legacy approaches to their unions. What they should have done was to force the union to stay at the table and to make increases dependent on the union membership's "buy-in" to the total product being sold. Bad management on both sides? Perhaps, but clearly living in a reactive environment is not a sustainable situation.

THE GOAL

If the goal was to do away with unions in the U. S. the effort worked. Clearly, unions overstepped their bounds. But now that unions are being stripped of their power, are we better off as a country? Only time will tell. In the meantime, the destruction of unions contributed to the commoditization of the American work force. The bad union managers carry at least half of the burden for that occurrence.

To the detriment of union and non-union workers, unions failed to correct both the behavior and the perception, contributing to the commoditization movement. Union members did, after awhile, begin following the direction of the union which had a political motive having more to do with controlling the company than with seeing everyone was treated fairly with respect to wages, benefits and safety.

WHY TALK ABOUT UNIONS?

It is important to include unions in the discussion of a commoditized work force because they are such a large part of this nation's industrial revolution and its success. While it is true unions have outlived their usefulness for the most part, at one time they were critical to progress. As a result, I believe there are many lessons that may be learned from a study of unions both in history and in the future.

Unions set the standard for labor until around 1980. There were the usual things - wages, benefits, work hours, safety, even child labor. One of the things many may not remember, or choose to ignore, is the apprenticeships and other educational and training opportunities that unions helped create and maintain. There was a time when a master machinist title meant something to a workplace. Being a tradesman meant having worked enough to produce a skill not found in others.

Unions became the mouthpiece for the workforce in America. An agent of sorts, they negotiated on the worker's behalf on the issues with which they felt concerned. There was some detachment of the rank and file from the decision making. There was also a microcosm of the society in the politics and backdoor maneuvering that ensued as absolute power threatened to corrupt absolutely. When we look back, we also see that unions were a lobbying influence on the US Congress, Senate and even the President. The loss of this function may have been the single largest change in the union relationship with American society. With the loss of the union's power and lobbying voice, labor lost a significant part of their voice with the government. The working class had no idea they were losing such an important advocate. This is not to say unions were completely eliminated. There are still enormous segments of the U. S. still under union influence.

In 2013, the union membership rate--the percent of wage and salary workers who were members of unions--was 11.3 percent, the same as in 2012, the U.S. Bureau of Labor Statistics reported today. The number of wage and salary workers belonging to unions, at 14.5 million, was little different from 2012. In 1983, the first year for which comparable union data are available, the union membership rate was 20.1 percent, and there were 17.7 million union workers.

The data on union membership were collected as part of the Current Population Survey (CPS), a monthly sample survey of about 60,000 households that obtains information on employment and unemployment among the nation's civilian noninstitutional population age 16 and over.

Highlights from the 2013 data:

- Public-sector workers had a union membership rate (35.3 percent) more than five times higher than that of private-sector workers (6.7 percent).
- Workers in education, training, and library occupations and in protective service occupations had the highest unionization rate, at 35.3 percent for each occupation group.

- Men had a higher union membership rate (11.9 percent) than women (10.5 percent).
- Black workers were more likely to be union members than white, Asian, or Hispanic workers.
- Among states, New York continued to have the highest union membership rate (24.4 percent), and North Carolina had the lowest rate (3.0 percent).[32]

Now that unions are being dismissed in society, it is important to remember that with the dismissal comes a requirement not to continue to blame unions for their impact, whether or not you believe that impact to be negative on the American work force. It does no good to dwell on the past beyond taking notes about what happened in history.

The commoditization of the American workforce since the late 1990's has partially been as a result of the vacuum created when unions were demonized and moved aside. Workers were used to negotiations on pay rates, benefits and safety occurring automatically as unions did what they were paid to do - represent the workers in an organization. The hourly rate was a well established figure and was determined simply by offering the job. No negotiation on the part of the employee was necessary.

When people started being recognized as commodities, placement agencies began to take the place of unions. Initially called temporary agencies (or temp agencies), they pre-negotiated needs

[32] http://www.bls.gov/news.release/union2.nr0.htm

and tasks along with compensation, and then they went out and found the resources and negotiated their package, keeping the difference for themselves. This was simply a shift of a function unions had been performing for years.

This had the effect of cheapening the contribution of both skilled and non-skilled workers. It also set up the commoditization we see now. Those of us caught in that cycle realized we could make more money, enjoy similar benefits, and have the freedom to choose the types of work we decided to do and for whom we did it. Gone were the days of the tyrannical supervisor and the "dead end" job. Our ability to continually improve our employment focus allowed us to pick and choose. The unfortunate result has been commoditization and the lack of security that followed.

Why talk about unions? Because they were such a big part of America's labor history. We also need to point out that many of the unions have played a part in their own demise (whether they knew it or not). They may have actually been part of the conspiracy to drive American jobs out of the country as they became part of the crony capitalist society. Unions are in this book because they are in the history books.

COLLECTIVISM

The selection of the group over the individual has been a goal of the union movement. Pitting the needs of the working class collective against the profiteers of American industry became very popular. During the Civil Rights movement, many leaders of that era were found aligning themselves with the unions in their work to protect the collective.

As Democrats and Liberals leaned towards Socialism, unions became a very effective proponent and tool of the collectivism of the union movement. However, this moved unions into direct opposition with the Constitutional model that is the United States. Progressives began their work in the early 1960's. Lyndon Johnson initiated an expansive welfare program during this period. Unions supported these progressive efforts to create a permanent welfare state.

This would come back to haunt the movement later in their history as the collective began to attempt to impose its will on members and non-members of the unions. Unions worked well in the U.S. because of the liberty that came with a Constitutional government. As with many things, the strong moves towards collectivism supported by unions were moving the country away from the government that allowed union success in the first place.

POLITICAL ABANDONMENT

During its long history, the union movement enjoyed a rich and productive relationship with politicians, primarily with the Democratic Party. Many election outcomes were determined based entirely on unions advocating for specific candidates; most of those candidates were Democrats. It was well known which unions supported which candidates. Once elected, those politicians returned the favor.

About the time of the PATCO challenges, some Democrats began to re-assess their long standing relationships with the unions. Ronald Reagan beat the Air Traffic Controllers handily, and with large popular support. Some politicians continued to see this as an opportunity to distance themselves from the unions.

The unions failed to recognize this situation. They also failed to recognize that their harsh, often confrontational approach was scaring people away from union membership.

At some point, politicians began walking a line between the need for votes and the cost of paying back the unions for their advocacy. Many simply chose not to stick with that part of their constituencies.

It is clear the Democrat Party has moved toward abandoning labor, and some could say the middle class, as they stopped being the advocate of manufacturing, jobs and the middle class. Beginning in the 1980's, the politics of unions took a different direction, pushing the U. S. directly toward commoditization. Who among the American citizen believes that organized labor would have allowed the mass export of jobs that has occurred since 1980? Who of us believes that commoditization would have occurred without union representation being involved? Yet here we are. Evidence enough that politicians are no longer a friend to labor.

A PRODUCTION BASED SOCIETY?

While the negative attitudes towards labor and labor unions did initially result in a backlash against labor and loosen labor markets somewhat, it also caused American companies to begin slowly moving production operations to other countries. One could argue that the work against unions simply became a distraction from the root cause, the need for additional profits that would come from the export of production work to other countries.

In an economic sense, this began to de-stabilize the American Dream. The American Dream was made possible because we were a production based society. The manufacturing of American consumer goods, and to some extent, services, made the country safe as a self-contained unit. People with many more credentials than me have proposed that America's move from a production based society is a natural one and will allow the country to move on to its next place in the world - that of leader and innovator. Frankly, I am unable to make the connection.

The United States is no longer a production based society. That being the case, what is the future role of unions? It is not clear in many cases what the value of services is compared to goods. Certainly, those services have been monetized to an international standard far below that of domestic services. The same is true for products.

When we were producing parts and manufactured items, it was easy to be a production based society. If it is true we have became a primarily services based society, the need for unions, as well as the resources they managed and had access to, has disappeared. Will the pendulum swing back over time? It is hard to say. The world is a very tentative place. The future is hard to imagine with the fluid world situation that exists today. Certainly, unions will be a part of that future world. Even in places like Poland, history has seen labor organized to right some wrong against the working class. Will American laborers return to organized labor? I propose commoditization makes that move inevitable. Will it be unionized? Who knows? The commoditized worker is closer to needing organized labor than it might appear.

PROGRESSIVISM

The Progressive movement used the collective tendency of unions toward socialism to further their left leaning agenda.

Beginning with the Depression, there have been forces at work developing methods for U. S. citizens to retire. Starting with Social Security, which was originally purely insurance, citizens of the U. S. were led to believe they were entitled to a retirement.

Later, the finance industry decided they could capitalize on this need for retirement by developing products that could deliver retirement for citizens over a long term.

With the cooperation of unions, corporate America and the U. S. government, the creation of 401k, IRA, and other financial instruments became prevalent, offering citizens methods for investing in order to provide a long term stipend for their retirement.

Each of these methods are really a means to finance a person's retirement. When unions were more prevalent, a person's life cycles were more structured, so it was taken for granted a person would have retirement at the end of their career and their life.

In May 2014, fifty percent of respondents to a Gallup poll felt they would have a comfortable retirement.[33]

However, in October 2013, thirty seven percent of respondents to a Wells Fargo survey indicated they would work until they die.[34]

TEMP AGENCIES

In 2013, it was announced that Kelly Services, a temp agency, had become the second largest employer in the U. S. This situation confirmed that unions had lost their effectiveness. Kelly has taken on the assignment of negotiation of value for workers.

Adding to the active anti-union effort by the U. S. government was the corporations and media. It did not help that unions took a combative approach to the primary issues.

What could have been done differently? One could argue that this fight needed to happen.

Are unions a thing of the past? It is hard to tell. As the American economy recovers, it remains to be seen if the lessons of unions have been learned. If American manufacturing recovers, how will the parties reach a common goal? How will that relationship look in the future? What role can/should a union play in the workforce today? There are many opinions. Commoditization of labor has changed the United States – possibly forever and irretrievably.

---

[33] http://www.gallup.com/poll/168959/americans-think-retire-comfortably.aspx

[34] https://www08.wellsfargomedia.com/downloads/pdf/com/retirement-employee-benefits/insights/2013-retirement-study.pdf

Unions, in their collective bargaining process, represented the workers in determining what it would cost to have their services in place for a company. That process included the worker, who expected the union to get them the maximum compensation possible for their effort.

Temp agencies have removed the employee from the conversation. Essentially, temp agencies are "selling" the talents generically, advising the individual what the company is willing to pay for the effort. Thus, the labor itself has become a commodity. It follows that the human resources are therefore commoditized.

WILL UNIONS EVER GAIN CONTROL AGAIN?

It is unlikely that unions will ever have as much control and power as they once did. One more reason that commoditization has occurred is the tendency of each person (commodity) to negotiate their own value in the economy. The collective bargaining model would try to negotiate on behalf of classes of workers; commoditized workers do not fit that model.

It is interesting that in 2014 an election was held for representation of Volkswagen employees in their plant in Chattanooga. It was not an enormous defeat of the UAW, but it was a defeat nonetheless. Even with VW's neutrality in the vote, employees voted 60% not to unionize.

It is also interesting to note that political pressure on the vote was enormous. Politicians threatened to withdraw tax benefits if the union was voted in. One politician even indicated VW would manufacture a sport utility vehicle in the plant if the employees rejected the union. The general manager of the facility immediately stated the union vote had nothing to do with the decision to increase manufacturing.

NO LONGER NEEDED?

Employees see no need for representation by an entity which many of them view as corrupt and unnecessary. As one official has said of the effort to organize a new Volkswagen manufacturing plant in Chattanooga: "If the UAW cannot organize the plant in Chattanooga, where can they organize?" Indeed. Unions got their start almost as soon as the first production line opened at Ford Motor Company. Combined with the efforts of Pinkerton Security, Ford worked with Pinkerton to ensure the plants did not close. Early in the history of Ford, there was some pretty abusive behavior, to the point that some workers were killed in the process. The Teamsters, and later the Autoworkers, were quite effective at gaining rules and work practices that ensured worker safety, treatment, pay and benefits. Some of that came at the hand of the government.

TRAINING

Unions worked hard to ensure members received adequate training and work experience to ensure their trade was being grown on a larger level. The apprentice was also seeing him/her - self improving and becoming more of a journeyman over time. This training and "slow cooking" of tradesmen (and tradeswomen) allowed for a constant stream of heavily qualified workers coming in to fill the need of the labor market. With the advent of retail education, is it possible the education system went along with the demonization of unions because they perceived an opportunity to profit from the elimination of apprenticeship programs?

INCLUSION

As a member of the Union, I was often amazed at how the janitors, house cleaners and others were treated by the company. It was as if they were somehow second hand contributors for their work. Clearly, theirs was a somewhat menial task, but those who showed up for work every day and whose presence was evident even when they were not "at work" has very well defined value to add to the effort. Over time, we somehow decided that anyone engaged in cleaning, then in repetitive tasks, then in semi-skilled trades such as bricklayer, carpenter or painter somehow provided less value than a tradesman, rather than seeing them as tradesmen. Or was it that the retail factor was already in place; less so I can live better. Why was their contribution worth so much less than the tradesmen who had completed a full apprenticeship or trade program? In my view, the value of all workers is most evident when they are not there, think of your garbage collector. When do you appreciate him most? When he either doesn't show up or a replacement comes instead. Even in the 1960's and 1970's, commoditization of some trades was already occurring.

Remember, commoditization is the norm in a capitalist society. If we were ever going to move from a monetized to a commoditized labor force, the unions would need to be removed from the equation. As we developed as a society, we began listening to media reports of abusive union contracts. There were, and continue to be, plenty of examples of overbearing and abusive unions who took advantage of their roles as representatives of their members. We will talk about this later as well.

IS COMMODITIZATION THE UNION'S FAULT?

Eventually we saw the big corporations begin to more openly blame unions for their failing or less than profitable companies. The media and politicians, even the Democrats who were supposedly the friends of labor, began to demonize unions and their members. The unions became the whipping boys for all things negative in corporate operations throughout the country. Questions about how the company was being run and what impact executive and management decisions had on the company's profitability became secondary to the impact the unions were having. Once again, American companies chose to be reactive rather than choose a proactive method of dealing with unions. As a society, we began to behave like victims. Regardless of which side you are on, it is clear that some of the companies were not being run as well as they should have been. It is possible the union was simply an easy excuse, or a distraction, for management.

As a root cause, no one bothered to consider that the unions had failed to make a needed paradigm shift. The unions themselves seemed to be oblivious to that need for change. We will discover why that happened later in the book as well.

This attitude began the division of the workforce into two classes, union and non-union workers. The division drove an already contentious battle between union members and those willing to cross a picket line to a new level. Instead of labor being united against management, labor was now distracted by the internal battle between themselves. Media, politicians and big business were actively demonizing the unions. In some cases, this was justified. But it was clearly a large distraction that would be integral in the commoditization of labor. It also appears to be a planned attack. It is not clear if media, politicians, big business and banks collaborated in the demonization of unions, but the effect was the same as if they had. Is commoditization caused by the unions? In some cases, it was. As a part of the larger effort to reduce or eliminate union influence, commoditization had to be the outcome.

DIVIDE AND CONQUER

In the book "It's OK to Leave the Plantation", the author points out methods slave owners used to keep people divided. In this case, it is possible that government and big business collaborated to divide labor by pointing out the worker who made a good hourly wage and had benefits as the enemy of the worker who did not have this option. Once the working class was divided, they were subject to overstepping government, finance and education because the union lobbies no longer had as much power. The Democrat Party simply turned its back on part of the union movement and left them to flounder. It is true that some politicians, primarily Democrats, still claim to be proponents of pro-labor policy, but the results do not bear that out.

Some would argue that the unions still have considerable power over the Democrat Party. I disagree. While I do recognize that some unions have some power, I believe that power is no longer originating in any sort of mutual agreement. Rather, the unions themselves have become commoditized and the relationship between the union and all politicians is now reduced to having been commoditized.

As the media, politicians, companies and even some labor continued to blame organized labor, sometimes justifiably, the manufacturing and services sector in the country took a large hit from international markets. As unions, organized labor, and American workers, both union and non-union, were sitting on the sidelines, they began to see jobs leaving the United States and headed for other countries. Worker's pay rates began to "equalize" with the foreign markets. Why would Wal-Mart pay four dollars for a shirt they could have manufactured in Taiwan for seventy five cents? Why would GM pay two hundred dollars for a transmission manufactured in Dearborn when they could get that same transmission from Mexico for thirty five dollars?

A job manufacturing parts in the U.S. paying fourteen dollars an hour, with benefits, safety, environmental consideration could be sent to Mexico to a facility hiring workers for one dollar an hour, with no benefits, and no environmental or safety regulation. The company could manufacture the parts in Mexico, ship them to the United States (with no tariff) and pocket the difference. No unions to deal with and less, if any, taxes to pay.

The American worker seemed to be OK with this for quite awhile until the Wal-Mart factor set in. We'll talk about that phenomenon later in this book as well.

This is where internationalization will not work. Each country has a system that contains economic, social and regulatory components. Those components are generally unique to that country. When importing and exporting, unless the entire system is traded, one country gains an advantage over another country. Sometimes these can be equalized with import or export tariffs. But generally speaking, ordering parts from Mexico was taking advantage of a poorer country and supplementing the system of that country.

Consider the recent clothing manufacturing in India - where over 1000 clothing workers were killed working in a textile plant. When considering the low cost, how many Americans are not bothered by the fact that human beings are working in a facility where they could be killed making clothes that Americans wear? I doubt many Americans have considered this question when watching American jobs leave the country, or when they walk into the discount chains that pervade this country.

The union movement that once served the country so well was now sitting on the sidelines. Sufficiently demonized and destroyed, they, much like the companies they were serving, were now in reactive mode as well. This left the American labor force to fend for themselves.

This is the root of the commoditized work force today. It has changed the core of the United States. In some cases, unions kept us together as a people. As a group, unions offered a common goal in the community, ensured a livable wage, and were very protective of those jobs in the American work force. Without that common bond, America has become more divided and factionalized as each person acting as a commodity is competing with every other person for their livelihood.

I realize this is an odd place for a Constitutionalist to be. I believe in free agency and in a free country. I believe in the right to self determination.

I also recognize the forces in place whose goal it is to keep the American citizens divided by whatever means necessary. The power of the unions was not the union itself. The power of the union was the common good that came from being united in providing a safe work environment, equitable pay and benefits, and a common belief that American workers produced world class products. The middle class and the working class were the beneficiaries of union efforts, whether they were union members or not. The middle class was protected by the strength of the working class. Without unions, there is no one left to defend the interests of the middle class. Or, at least, no one willing to listen........

This is a condition that can be fixed. Maybe not by bringing unions back, but by citizens uniting to create a common mode of making a living, advocating an ethical and moral standard, and deciding to support the country through economic means.

In an odd way, commoditization has replaced the unions. Those of us who are commoditized have found we are generally negotiating our compensation package on an ongoing basis. Recruiting companies assist us in determining the market rate of our skills and we each determine what we will and will not do for that compensation. Where we still lose is that there are a number of workers whose job is no longer needed in our society. Was this by design? One could argue that organized and unorganized labor participated in the transformation…….this transformation led to commoditization.

SUMMARY

The subject of unionization has always been controversial. Try for a moment to leave the emotions of that controversy behind as you consider the impact of unions on the commoditization of labor in the U. S.:

Unions gained enormous control over labor markets in the U. S.; even in the world markets. Their sometimes over reaching efforts to defend and advocate for labor fed the division that became their downfall. One could say the perception that unions had gotten too big and had too much power caused many to abandon the unions. However, not many people would argue that labor would have gone along with the relocation of almost all industries to foreign countries since the mid 1980s. The weakening of the unions weakened the labor markets, which was necessary in order to commoditize American workers.

Unions were an annoyance to businesses and government in many ways. One of the most obvious annoyances was unions having control over labor, one of the larger cost components of manufactured goods. By virtue of their control of the cost of labor, they were received as a negative influence on the profitability of manufacturing companies throughout the country. While they were large political donors and controlled enormous retirement funds, politicians slowly abandoned the union movement partially out of pragmatism and partially because of their enormous political power had become a liability to the professional politician.

There can also be no question that unions forgot about the people they were supposed to serve. Much like the politicians in the U. S., union leaders forgot they take direction from the members they represent.

As a result, organized unions became the enemy of organized labor. Combined with the fact that the Democrat Party sold out the unions late in the twentieth century, the union "machine" is dying because of its lack of true leadership and failure to recognize how collective bargaining should work.

One necessary component of commoditization was to weaken labor's collective size and sense of common purpose. Another was to weaken their political control. This could have only happened by creating and fostering a negative image of organized labor. Did the unions do this to themselves? Or were they pushed off the cliff, victims of a decades long setup engineered by big government, big business and big finance in order to move these industries to locations more favorable to profitable manufacturing? I propose they did it to themselves, and to the rank and file members. Sure, big government, big business and big money have benefited from the demise of unions, but the rank and file allowed unions to get out of control, thus turning the page on an important phase in history.

CONCLUSIONS

Unions contributed to commoditization for a variety of reasons. Unlike the other components, not many of the unions contributed to commoditization for their own benefit. The union's contribution was more through the poor execution that caused union usefulness, authority and power to be diminished.

After the Democrat Party turned their backs on the union movement, abandoning the ideals they had defended for so long, unions were left wandering for awhile. This wandering gave the advantage to big companies, big banks and big governments. Along with the other special interests mentioned these interests strengthened the retail economy in The U. S. and almost guaranteed the success of efforts to commoditize labor and the workers who provided it.

Chapter 6

Legal Systems

LAWYERS

Attorneys in America had enormous impact on manufacturing, consumption, product selection, healthcare, government and many other issues. "The trouble with the law is lawyers." **Clarence Darrow**

As I have mentioned before, in a capitalist society, everything is retail. Supply and demand are often used to determine the value and importance of our labors. Lawyers have a unique opportunity. They have managed to protect their right to charge for their time. In many cases they get paid whether they win, or lose.

Lawyers sometimes create turmoil. Lawyers sometimes resolve turmoil. In many cases, they are on both sides of an issue. This places them in a position to influence American lives in many ways, all of them in ways that enrich the lawyer.

LITIGATION

In our litigious society, we have discovered that almost everything is subject to legal action. Whether deliberate or accidental, some attorneys have discovered a way to bring suit for almost any incident that occurs. Many of us live in fear of being sued. Many individuals and businesses have changed their lives and processes to ensure they are not subjecting themselves to legal risk. If we are fortunate enough, we can buy insurance to protect against litigation in the event we become party to a lawsuit.

LEGISLATION FROM THE BENCH

Many people live for the opportunity to win their case in court. Lawyers want rulings in their favor. But the legal system is supposed to allow for impartial judgment and interpretation of the law.

The Constitution provides for a separation of powers. The three branches of government, legislative, legal and executive, each have areas designated to them. However, sometimes a judge will make a ruling against a standing law. Sometimes a judge will rule in a way favorable to a different law. When this occurs, the legal system is said to be "legislating from the bench". In other words, judges are writing and passing law by virtue of their power as jurist in the legal branch.

This can be problematic because it leaves out the influence of the voter and of the legal authority granted only to the Congress to create and implement law.

AMBULANCE CHASERS?

From product liability, to bad behavior, to simple accidents, the retail legal system has created a class of people who exist to prey on those who encounter those incidents.

The term "ambulance chaser" is a term used to describe those in the legal profession who would pursue "victims" of these incidents in the hope of selling them something. Since in this form law is a retail commodity, it would be understanding that a lawyer might chase an ambulance in the chance that there would be an opportunity to peddle his wares, legal advice, insulation from a lawsuit, or the possibility of receiving a reward for having been damaged or injured.

JAILS AND THE PRISON SYSTEM

In years past, the country and the world have experienced a more pragmatic approach to crime and punishment. In the U. S., being in the prison system was not a very pleasant experience. As punishment, that was the point of prisons.

At some point, the idea of rehabilitation occurred. While this seemed a very good idea, it injected a level of difficulty and trust that might be unrealistic. This changed our jails and prisons from purely punitive to retail penal institutions. One could argue that the opportunity to sell the prison experience might create a conflict of interest between legislators and the prison system.

Consider crime and punishment today. Crime does not necessarily stop the behavior just because the particular crime has been made illegal.

INCARCERATION RATES

In this day and age, the U. S. has the highest incarceration rate of any government on the planet. Over 2.4 million people are currently incarcerated across the United States. The State of Louisiana has the highest incarceration rate in the world.

It can be argued that the for profit prison industry accounts for at least some of the high incarceration rates. Along with the U. S. drug war and mandatory minimum sentencing, the criminalization of human behavior contributes to commoditization by placing a large segment of the population in retail prisons. One could question whether privatization of prisons and jails places governments and the prison companies themselves in a conflict of interest. How can a company that makes its revenue running prisons lobby a government for "customers" and not have an influence on long term prison population? How can that same company be paced in charge of an entire population of citizens whom they are charged with rehabilitating?

I have personal experience in this subject. I have one son who has spent time in the prison system. He has been incarcerated almost as much as he has been free. Most of the incarceration has been caused by bad decision making on his part.

When he has been out of jail, on a few occasions he has indicated he missed incarceration. His logic is that he is well cared for and that he has less pressure and stress in his life. One could see how he could come to this conclusion.

LEGISLATORS

In years past, the country and the world operated under the assumption that representative government would operate under the premise of honesty and ethical decision making. As the legal system has matured, it has influenced many who have conflicts of interest. Many legislators make poor choices based on the action of lobbyists and others.

From The American Bar Association:

As the number of Americans incarcerated for low-level, nonviolent offenses has increased, so has the number of private prisons. In 1990, only a few years after private prisons first began to proliferate, 7,000 prisoners were housed in private facilities nationwide. In June 2010, the number rose to 126,000 prisoners, or 9 percent of the nation's total state and federal prison population. In recent years, tremendous growth in private prisons has occurred on the federal level, particularly in the area of immigration detention. However, 2011 marked a renewed push toward expanding private prisons on the state level.

As the number of private prisons has grown, it has also led to banner profits for the companies. The largest private prison company, Corrections Corporation of America (CCA), reported revenues of $1.675 billion in 2010 alone.

Again from The American Bar Association:

The Power of The Private Prison Lobby

… the private prison company uses its relationships and resources to create the most favorable environment for it to earn a profit. The result is a culture of corruption where state officials support and enact policies that will enhance the profits of the private prisons. While this is beneficial for the company, it often comes at the expense of the taxpayer, who must pay more for an

expanding prison system and to incarcerate people who would be better served in a less expensive community corrections setting.[35]

SUMMARY

The War on Drugs started in the 1980s has contributed to a failed policy tried previously during prohibition. The opportunities for profit and an expanded government have contributed to the commoditization of the American workforce by idling large segments of the population in for-profit jails and prisons, some privately run and some run by governments.

I once had a conversation with one of my sons who had spent time in prison. While he was out and was progressing, he would often tell me how he missed the "three hots and a cot". A study of recidivism rates in the US reveals the number of prisoners returning is significant. It is easy to conclude then that this system encourages people to become dependent on the government for their support rather than encouraging them to take care of themselves.

CONCLUSIONS

In order to resolve the commoditization issue, we must first look at criminalization of behavior in America. As with all "sins", we must resist the tendency to criminalize these behaviors and the

---

35 http://www.americanbar.org/publications/human_rights_magazine_home/human_rights_vol38_2011/human_rights_summer11/prisons_for_profit_incarceration_for_sale.html

temptation to build a large government infrastructure to deal with the results.

In discussing the overgrown prison system, we need to segregate behaviors. For those who place society in immediate danger (murder, bodily harm, property destruction, etc), a more harsh, less lavish punishment would be in order.

For those behaviors which would fall in the category of self harm or simply a bad decision, we must first decide if the process of making such behavior illegal has any impact. Once we decide it has very little impact (ie – speeding tickets relative to public safety) we would want to look at transferring these behaviors to correction through a higher social code or some other method.

Our legal system plays a part in the commoditization because their services have become commoditized as well. And the profession has discovered it can generate revenue from a commoditized population.

Chapter 7

Education

Education in the United States has been divided into two primary parts. Both of them are essentially government run institutions. Even the privately held schools are subject to state and federal oversight designed to fit the assimilation and indoctrination efforts of government.

PUBLIC PRIMARY EDUCATION

The first part, public education, has unquestionably done a very poor job of providing the nation's youth with the most basic education. As one examines the role of government funded public education, it becomes apparent the under-performing public education system may have simply become a glorified day care system. With Common Core, No Child Left Behind, Race To The Top and the multitude of other social engineering projects, the federal government has been paying local (state run) schools to adapt to and adopt lower intellectual standards.

There can be no question the public schools have largely become a tool for assimilation and indoctrination. There is some difference of opinion as to the purpose of that indoctrination.

In addition, public education's attempts to redefine society in a number of ways has simply reduced the expectations of many and attempted to eliminate the Judeo Christian standards that were the basis of this great country. Redefining government's role in marriage, finance, education and families has masked the underlying problems with society.

Further, public education continues to use the format of conformance to a man-made standard. Everyone fitting in the box is labeled as "normal", everyone else is "abnormal" – ie ADD, ADHD, etc. This is not to say that some of these ailments are not real, but public education has become an enabler. Enabling its students to become victims of the myriad social "diseases" rather than enabling them to overcome whatever is perceived as "holding them back". This has the effect of scarring the labeled students. Negatively impacting their ability to achieve.

POST SECONDARY EDUCATION

The second part, secondary education, has become what I like to call "retail education". Much like buying a car, or a home, or a sack of groceries, the nation's colleges and universities have been focusing more efforts on selling education than on selling the RIGHT education, matched to the intellect and natural talents of those who are being pursued for enrollment. This is the commoditization of education necessary for the commoditization of labor. The total net cost of a post-secondary education has increased at a rate higher than inflation.[36]

In fact, higher education has increased in cost twice as fast as the

---

[36] http://nces.ed.gov/programs/coe/indicator_cua.asp

rate of growth in the cost of healthcare. [37]

Education is one of two American institutions that have managed to escape the societal elimination of unions. We have already established that unions have their own agenda and that when that agenda conflicts with the focus of the enterprise, the union's goals have historically won. Unlike almost every other industry, the union representation of educator has risen throughout the period from 1990 to 2010. There are many statistics regarding this period, but one of the more telling contained in a Cato Institute report is the increase in wages and the decrease in education quality. [38] Moreover, the potential for profit from education is enormous. There is no real motivation for the providers to ensure long term benefit from the education. Students generally have no idea how to assess their need, or the impact of their education on their future. A pure analysis of the return on investment (ROI) on most people's education would reveal enormous risk. Careers are getting shorter. Life cycles of technology are getting shorter. People are living longer. Combined with commoditization, the likelihood the education will have long term value for the student is not high. Of course, the most important aspect of investing in your future is to choose an appropriate education in a field that hopefully pays well. For instance, if you are left brained and pursue a degree in

---

[37] http://www.dailyfinance.com/on/college-costs-tuition-rising-student-debt-infographic/

[38] http://object.cato.org/sites/cato.org/files/serials/files/cato-journal/2010/1/cj30n1-8.pdf

engineering, you are far more likely to see a return on your investment than if you secure a degree in the arts. [39]

When we also consider the profit motive and its impact on education, we discover that the retail component of education has commoditized the education itself.[40] As a retail product, the generation of sales for the sake of sales or revenue overrides the importance of the impact of the product, making it difficult to determine the total value of the education. For instance, someone who might do quite well as a tradesman might be sold a much higher education than they need.

This is not to say one should not get an education. It simply points out that the individual must be prepared to do a better analysis of the desired impact of the education, along with a long term analysis of total return on investment. How many people do you know with a degree in a career field in which they no longer, or maybe never, worked? How many do you know who, like me, have watched their careers vanish behind some new technological discovery?

PUBLIC EDUCATION

What is it that has caused public education to become more about indoctrination and assimilation than development of intellect and knowledge over the last 50 to 60 years? Arguably, the

---

[39] http://www.economist.com/news/united-states/21600131-too-many-degrees-are-waste-money-return-higher-education-would-be-much-better

[40] http://www.centerforcollegeaffordability.org/uploads/For-Profit_corr_2.pdf

government's involvement has taken control of the message being delivered to our children. This in itself is not reason for alarm, but does cause some concern when we look at the fundamental change this causes in the American society.

Public education touches and has been touched by all facets of government. From basic curriculum, to the setting of social standards, to nutrition to the structure of a child's home, public educators have been increasingly involved in parenting the nation's children. Reduced to a glorified daycare center in some cases, they have been placed in the unenviable position of mass education of an enormous group of very diverse young people who have no idea where they want to go or what they want to do. In that regard, the ominous task of determining the future of each American child is in the hands of public education.

Combined with the extremely diverse background and experience of so many, the tendency to "teach down" is used to ensure everyone meets a standard, one standard that moves at the whim of the politicians who provide the funding for that education. Unfortunately, those who might achieve more are not pushed to achieve their full potential. The recognition of each individual as unique and deserving of refinement of those unique talents is nearly impossible as the measurement of intellect becomes more important than the distribution of intellect. Not everyone has the aptitude to be a doctor, lawyer, or mechanic, or any of the hundreds of career paths they might choose. My dad used to say "If you want to feed your family, be a plumber. Plumbers are never out of work."

Unfortunately, public education has become less about the individual and more about the collective. The young minds are tested, and then re-tested in order to determine what they know in order to determine if they "conform" to the testing "standards". However, no testing is done to see what their natural talents, their aptitude and personality, reveal. The government-run education system falls victim to a program designed to measure the immeasurable. As a consequence, the standards of public education get caught in an effort to force all children into the same mold. In a race to the least common denominator, American public education does a poor job of preparing children and teens for participation in the world as individuals, instead working to prepare them all to be the same.

When considering the root cause of this condition, the government once again receives most of the blame. Very few, if any, government programs are effective or efficient in achieving their desired goals. As government has engaged in "everyone in the box" education, many have fallen out of the mold to be labeled with such ominous terms as attention deficit hyperactivity disorder (ADHD) or attention deficit disorder (ADD). Segregated from other students, these children grow up to be the unfortunate victims of social engineering and the inability of a government program about to collapse in on itself because of its enormity and inefficiency. It is not often that we hear that public education's approach might simply not be challenging children in a way that fits their natural talents and/or aptitudes. There is a quote from Michael J. Fox: "If a child can't learn the way we teach, maybe we should teach the way they learn."

In terms of cost to government and society in general, the cost per student is extremely high given the output. I do not say this to support the idea that we should simply throw more money at the problem. In fact, I think an analysis shows the opposite should occur. Application of efficiency and better processes would bring more value to public education. Like most government programs, spending money on the program would only spend more money. Nothing more.[41] Even with the slight decrease in spending in 2011, the cost per student is very high and provides no real measurement of value and/or effectiveness of the programs being purchased.

In any regard, when children enter college or secondary training, they are ill prepared for the tasks they need to accomplish. Since "retail education" in post-secondary education can charge for the remedial training needed to make up for the training not received in public schools, the young people (or their parents) initially spend their money getting the person caught up rather than moving them forward. Since much of the post-secondary education is borrowed, one could argue that many Americans are borrowing money in order to pay for what they or their parents already paid for, but did not receive from their taxpayer funded education.

[41] http://nces.ed.gov/fastfacts/display.asp?id=66

ORGANIZED EDUCATION FACILITIES

I believe the causes for our under-performing education system began in the 1960's when some education facilities began looking for the "profit motive" in some specializations. There is a significant history in education. The entire education system has been a pawn of sorts, becoming subject to influence and interference from government, banks, and educators themselves. Unfortunately, the people who got into the education business did not always provide a great product. There were not clear measures of the end product, sometimes; simply obtaining a certificate or degree was not an indicator of a person's ability to perform the work. I know many educators who are quite good at teaching, but have been hamstrung by over reaching administrative, political or financial interference from programs such as No Child Left Behind or even the new Common Core.[42]

In my opinion, this came from a lack of adequate preparation of the person being educated. Since the 1960's, public schools have been providing more testing, indoctrination and assimilation as they work to put everyone inside the box that is standardized testing. Without some accommodation for aptitude, natural talent and level of interest, choosing a person's career path will likely be

[42] http://whatiscommoncore.wordpress.com/tag/teachers-against-common-core/

an elusive exercise.[43]

The entire United States public education system (K - 12) is a bloated, inefficient and ineffective machine bent on compliance and the assimilation of free thinkers. The killing of innovation, free thought and individuality is evident in the setting of lower standards, lack of adequate or appropriate assessment of students, assignment of blame and development of new excuses for poor performance disguised as new diseases. Obama's divisive government, combined with his "philosophy of can't" make the product of public education more about victimhood than about individual achievement.

While ADD and ADHD might be legitimate and well founded diseases for a few people in the education system, I believe the true cause in some cases is the inability of the education system to identify a curriculum that is equally challenging for all students, recognizing each student's unique capabilities for contribution. "If a child does not learn the way we teach, maybe we should teach the way they learn?"

The result of public education for those who see things differently is boredom and lackluster performance causing poor behavior and a lack of excitement. Many of these students are simply being bored into submission. Over-diagnosis of ADHD is rampant in a government run healthcare system that has mandated it as an

---

[43] http://www.huffingtonpost.com/2014/01/10/common-core_n_4537284.html

excuse. It is a government run disability program that uses ADHD as a qualifier for Social Security Disability – even for grownups as old as fifty! Who of us has not known someone who has suffered a personal tragedy that placed them on disability? I know many people who have been diagnosed with ADHD, some of them getting the first diagnosis in their thirties. It is simply systematic misery. To the contrary, I know many people who have overcome those maladies and been successful despite the "disease".

The United States education system was a co-conspirator in the social engineering experiment that produced the commoditization of people. First, no one in K-12 is really watching for a student's natural talent. I am but one example, having been put on track for something in music while in the fourth grade. Why? I haven't a clue other than it was easy for me and kept me busy. I became a C average student all the way through high school, barely passing classes and almost missing the opportunity to graduate. In hindsight, I was allowed to be lazy because the school could not find what interested me (other than girls and cars). I would go to class, make a C, and then skip classes until the next class, hanging out in the band room most of the time.

The music diversion also contributed to my becoming a less than average performer. I was always first or second chair trombonist, always attended music events, always went to try outs, football games and other music events, but always was a mid C student. No one approached me to be or do more. (Arguably my parents should have done that – but they did not.)

You can read about my entry into the Air Force in my book, "From The Strip Club To The Temple". The primary thing I got from that experience was the results of the armed services vocational aptitude battery (ASVAB) test. I was totally surprised when, at age 25, the results of that test revealed I was a candidate for electronics training at Chanute Air Force Base. The question would be why after a "career" in high school and some college pursuing a degree in music, it was news to me that my talents were not in music, but in electronics. Could it be that the education system was not capable of determining the strengths and weaknesses of my personal skills? The switch from right brained to left brained activities was a pivotal moment in my life. How unfortunate I had to wait twenty five years to become aware of my real aptitude.

In my military career I went on to complete seven months of electronics training with extremely high scores. I advanced to E4 in record time and was honorably discharged from the military as a result of the "up or out" program as a technical sergeant (TSGT) (E6) after ten years of service.

I have since obtained a degree in avionics. That field virtually vaporized before my eyes when the aviation industry imploded and the technology life cycle caught up with my career. Fortunately, I did obtain a background in technology that has served me well. But it was not from an education facility. Rather, it was from a workplace, or a group of workplaces, where I was mentored in the industry in which I am now employed. Arguably, I received training very similar to the training unions had been providing years ago. For some people mentoring often produced better opportunities than a formal education. From an ICU nurse to a physician to fellow IT workers, I was allowed to make a few mistakes, granted the wisdom of those mentors and ultimately trusted by clients to help them in their business operations.

Had I not taken the ASVAB, I might still not be aware of my tendency to left brained activity. Throughout the twelve years of early school through a couple of years in music in college, no one ever noticed what a single recruiter noticed from a single test of a twenty five year old. Why is that?

Certainly, without the ASVAB, and the U.S. Air Force, I would not have gained access to my consulting career. I am amazed how much difference that one event made. How many people never have that one moment? I propose the numbers are staggering.

STUDENT LOAN PROGRAMS (BANKS)

The Federal Government set up student loans years ago in a series of staged events on the way to retail education. Today, these loans have made college degrees another commodity, and made the degrees worth less in the process.[44]

In so doing they became complicit in manipulating that market through a series of kickbacks, incentives and other programs. These questionable loans are choking people and contribute to the

---

[44] http://www.againstcronycapitalism.org/2014/08/how-government-made-your-college-degree-worth-less-a-lot-less/

profit motive at the aforementioned education facilities.[45] [46]

The banks engaged in Federal Student Loan programs handed out the money, and were the beneficiary of a wide variety of fees and charges; many to the financial benefit of the banks. Schools received "incentives" for referrals. These referrals were pure profit for education facilities.

Refinance packages made banks even more money as they:

1) Allowed higher interest financing
2) Allowed bundling of loans
3) Obfuscated the complete history of student loans.

Combined with changing the law to remove the ability to discharge student loans in bankruptcy, these package deals are close to servitude as they saddle students with tens, sometimes hundreds, of thousands of dollars in debt.

I personally still owe over sixty thousand dollars on student loans for an Associate's Degree I received in 1988. The potential that my children will wind up paying these loans is quite high.

Debtor's prisons do still exist in the form of non-dischargeable debt obtained in an effort to gain more predictable employment. Now that employment has been commoditized, what is the hope of the person borrowing one hundred thousand dollars in order to get

---

[45] http://www.usnews.com/news/articles/2013/10/01/student-loan-default-rates-rise-for-sixth-year

[46] http://www.slate.com/articles/business/moneybox/2014/04/student_loan_profits_the_government_makes_its_money_off_grad_students.html

a career? What guarantees do they have that investment will result in a solid and dependable means for repaying the loans?

FROM TCAP TO COMMON CORE

In 2013 there began a new federal mandate to "improve" education in the United States. The federal government created and mandated a new program titled, "Common Core". Common Core was advertised as state run education. It has been implemented by state education departments, but is financed by the federal government. In fact, the federal government claims it is a state run initiative. If buying off state governors is the definition of state led, then they are correct. A program that is clearly filled with misleading data, it has revealed questionable, required teaching methods. Focusing almost entirely on measurement, it grills students throughout their learning careers, casting aside the non-conforming and leaving behind a stack of underperforming drones incapable of free thought or initiative.

ASSIMILATION

On Star Trek, it was the Borg ("You Will Be Assimilated"). In Orwell's 1984, it was Big Brother ("Free Thinking Will Not Be Tolerated"). In Pink Floyd's The Wall, it is the maniacal teacher ("If You Don't Eat Your Meat, You Can't Have Any Pudding !"). Today, it is Common Core. The public education system has become a tool of the government, assimilating the citizens and their children into all being the same.

In Pink Floyd's “The Wall”, the students, all unique and individual, walk down a conveyor belt into a meat grinder, emerging as tiny, little faceless clones.

In Hitler's youth program, the assimilation included the annihilation of an entire race of people.

In August 2012, the Washington Post said this: *It's a bad idea. Ignore the fact that specific* Common Core State Standards *will open up enough cans of worms to keep subject-matter specialists arguing among themselves forever.*[47]

I encourage you to research the subject to make up your own mind. Clearly, the federal government is taking a much more active role in the education of our children. My concerns are similar to the concerns in the Washington Post article;

there does not appear to be any accommodation for a person's individual traits such as aptitude, personality, individual interest or, certainly, free thinking

The U. S. government has injected itself into the education of citizens in a continuation of its ongoing efforts to force behavior since free will has caused the citizens to ask too many questions. One solution would be for parents to take a more active role in speaking with their children, and engaging them in conversations to fill in the gaps, or correct the modified or incomplete histories being given them in public school. This would require the parents becoming proactive regarding their children's best interests, and

---

[47] http://www.washingtonpost.com/blogs/answer-sheet/post/eight-problems-with-common-core-standards/2012/08/21/821b300a-e4e7-11e1-8f62-58260e3940a0_blog.html

making appropriate prioritization of this very important family matter.

BANKS

Why mention banks in the education section of the book? Because banks are complicit in the commoditization process.

Banks are making money on student loans; lots of it! Just like other areas of the United States, Big Money, much of it outside the borders of the U. S. has stepped in to make money and capitalize on the opportunity wherever they may. In the case of student loans, banks cash in on them by providing loans to anyone who requests them regardless of the appropriateness of the education or the likelihood of success or completion of the curriculum.

As noted earlier, these loans are not dischargeable in bankruptcy. When exempted from bankruptcy, student loans became the closest thing to debtors prison this country has ever seen. Think of it; a person borrows $50,000.00 of long term debt (on which the interest and fees automatically capitalize) with absolutely no idea of how it will impact his or her future. The same government that provides the loans allows the economy to tank making it difficult, if not impossible, to pay the loans back. Since bankruptcy is no longer an option, the loan must be paid anyway.

There are also the deceptive "qualifications" to pass when applying for these loans. Not very stringent, the qualifications are to be alive, be a US Citizen and be enrolled or enrolling in a post-secondary education program.

There are forbearance and other consolidation programs for students while actively attending schools. There are consolidation packages after a student completes their education. In all of these cases, the opportunities for banks to profit are almost endless. There are fees for the transactions, fees for the loans, fees for the banks, and fees for the schools. Even when filing for bankruptcy, the loan accrues interest during the non-payment period.

Yes, you can get forbearance or a deferral. Yes, you can catch up your loan over time. But read the fine print. The punitive measures surrounding those programs end up with the student loan holder acting as the payday loan guy, taking every opportunity to invoke the fine print version of fees in order to make it worth their while to service the loan.

In all of these transactions, the student rarely has a formula for calculating the true return on investment for their student loans. Sure, if a student is successful at gaining a loan in a field for which they have the aptitude and may become qualified, the ROI is less risky. But what if the student has no aptitude for the subject matter? Or what if technology life cycles eliminate the career before the student pays off the loans? What is the risk in obtaining a degree that might be obsolete in a shorter time frame than the student loans?

THE GOVERNMENT (AGAIN)

The United States Government has decided that everyone needs a degree in order to become a "success". Who says everyone has to have a college education? The government. Why? Reading this book should make the motivations pretty clear.

While some would that the U. S. is moving to a service based economy, many think this means service in technology. If you want to have a long term career, be a plumber. People with skills in the trades (carpenter, plumber, auto mechanic, etc) have been supporting themselves and their families for years. Those people providing service can do so without obtaining an advanced education.[48]

An additional theory is that public education has done such a poor job that many are having to get a college degree to simply get the same education one formerly received in order to obtain a high school diploma.[49] Government inefficiency and ineffectiveness in education has caused us to have to supplement a high school education with additional education beyond that expected from government run schools. That education is being performed at additional expense to the taxpayer.

SUMMARY

The education systems in the United States have been nationalized. Whether we agree with the concept of public education or not, there is no question that allowing government to determine the content of the education allows those governments to treat public

---

[48] http://education-portal.com/articles/Does_Everyone_Really_Need_a_College_Degree.html

[49] http://www.highereducation.org/reports/college_readiness/gap.shtml

education as an opportunity to indoctrinate.

These systems also produce multiple opportunities for profit. In these efforts, many companies line up for the opportunity to profit from public education.

Education contributes to commoditization by promoting the collective efforts of government and by advocating for itself.

CONCLUSIONS

Consider with me that the United States government no longer has the best interests of its citizens in mind when regulating, taxing and financing education in this country. It is clearly a conflict of interest to be the sole advocate of a policy, especially when that idea comes from the government.

For the last 45 years, the Department of Education of the United States, and many state education departments, has been more engaged in assimilation and indoctrination than in true education. With very little consideration for a person's background, core talents, left or right brained capability, or even desire, public education from pre-K through high school and into college has worked to drive students into a well defined, monolithic approach to education. Rather than develop intellect in our students, we measure their ability to spew back data spewed to them just days or weeks earlier. This method, teaching the test, is more common now as state governments need the test measures to be able to prove the effectiveness of their approach to education.

While the intent might not be assimilation in the sinister sense, it is certainly assimilation in the sense that cattle must be herded into a gated area.

The demand for public education is enormous. But is it truly necessary to have a degree in order to succeed? What of the trades? Who will repair all the items that break in our society?

Even as education from the elementary through high school has failed our society, the expectation for two year degrees has gotten greater. Given the profit motive for providing that education, it can be no wonder that the assimilation programs have reduced much of public education to nothing more than a glorified daycare service.

What did education do to contribute to commoditization? I propose the impact is trifold:

1) Commoditization of education; education itself has been commoditized. In an attempt to develop and deploy a "one size fits all" education in K-12, education changed from having refinement and enhancement of the person to training the person to fit a predefined set of ideas.

2) Commercialization of education; throughout the education cycle, the retail education product has become more about sales than about ensuring the training and education fits the person purchasing the education.

3) Federal government education; the federal government has taken the responsibility for "public" education. In combination with some state governments, they have been free to define what education looks like. As government often does in these efforts, they have used the opportunity to distract students from what they need to develop skills and talents for a successful career. Instead,

government involvement made the focus on “changing” people, revising education, rewriting history, and reestablishing the definition of families, rather than training people in what they can do to refine their abilities.

These things contributed to the commoditization of the American workforce by contributing to the failure of education to partner with private industry and manufacturing.

How do we correct this situation? Get government out of the education business. Beginning with K-12, bring parents back into the discussion of what is best for their children, and work to give all parents access to that process

Chapter 8

Technology

Technology has played an important role in the commoditization of the American work force. The infrastructure of the United States now depends largely on many technologies to perform the underlying work necessary to support the large and very diverse population. There was a time when workers were hyper-sensitive to the replacement of jobs with technology. In the mid 1900's, much of that concern was dismissed. By the late 1900s, it had become clear that technology would have a large impact on American labor markets. The Y2K scare brought the impact of technology to the forefront as we mitigated issues with technology in critical places throughout society.

Many of the idle and repetitive tasks formerly performed by human resources are now performed by technology. Much of the work that required a strong infrastructure staffed by human resources has simply been out dated.

Think of the impact of technology on newspapers, magazines and other print media. Consider how technology has impacted payroll processing, healthcare billing, and engineering.

Computers have become commonplace in the world.[50] Look

[50] http://smallbusiness.chron.com/technology-impacting-changes-21st-century-workplace-3357.html

around and recognize the prevalence of technology in every stage of human life.[51] There are now even addictions associated with all of the technologies.[52]

THE IMPACT OF PORTABLE TECHNOLOGY

In the early days of technology, portable devices like the Palm device were prevalent. Largely just a contact manager and note taker, the device could be used to manage a person's contact database and capture those thoughts that occurred in inconvenient places.

In 1973, the first handheld telephone (cell phone) came on the market. In just forty years, the cell phone has become the primary mode of communications for many. For example, in 1985, there were 340,213 cell phone subscribers. By 2010, that number had ballooned to 300,520,098! In just 25 years, the number of subscribers grew by over 880%.[53]

The original cell phone was just as much a toy as it was a tool. Compared to other communications devices, it was a very cool thing to own. As the technology improved, cell phones became more essential. Since the year two thousand they have become increasingly capable multipurpose devices able to perform many

---

[51] http://www.cnbc.com/id/101581976#.

[52] http://www.huffingtonpost.com/jan-cloninger-and-rosemary-strembicki-lcsw/how-is-technology-affecting-your-family_b_3915849.html

[53] http://www.infoplease.com/ipa/A0933563.html

tasks once performed only manually.

Today, technology is much more robust and readily available in many forms. From online applications to phones that contain more power than some desktop computers, they are tools that make us more effective in a variety of ways.

One of the ways technology has had an impact is that many of us now do the work previously performed by a secretary or administrative assistant. In this way, technology has contributed to commoditization. Technology has brought efficiency and organization to many aspects of our society. But providing that has come at the sacrifice of service jobs previously associated with performing those functions.

Communications technology has changed the way each of us stays in touch. It also makes it possible for us to have more immediate access to a plethora of information and ways to go about task accomplishment.

REDEFINITION OF THE MALL

Technology helped to make some of the shopping malls in the U.S. less utilized. The redefinition of shopping malls was caused by a combination of the influencers described in this book, many of which have also caused the commoditization of the American worker. Shopping for many goods has become a regular event on the internet. Technology has made the world smaller.

SUMMARY

Technology allowed work forces to be commoditized by making

competitive marketing much more prevalent. It also allowed manufacturers to build products for markets that could never afford those products.

Technology has made the world smaller. It also allowed the message of new world order more prevalent. The commoditized technology has allowed a media machine to control what part of the smaller world we see and hear.

CONCLUSIONS

There may not really be much that can be done about the impact of technology on commoditized labor. The societal issues and the other influencers mentioned in this book have changed things to the point that going back is not possible. The function of the mall is being redefined. The small "mom and pop" stores are all but gone. The outlet mall appears to have survived in some form. Wal-Mart has replaced a large section of retail with a single store. What is needed is a clearer picture of where technology is going. We also need to encourage a workforce fully engaged in leveraging technology in order to have innovative thinking drive the future of technologies. In that process, it will take work to define what part technology plays in the commoditized worker's career and in their lives.

Chapter 9

The United Nations

The United Nations was created to bring together the nations of the world. In their zeal for one world government, they have placed the interests of their organization and all other governments other than United States above the interests of the United States.

It is possible the United Nations is in a peculiar conflict of interest. The UN receives over twenty five percent of its funding from the United States. Its headquarters is in New York City. Its leaders live in America. Yet their world view and need for control places their purpose clearly in that conflict.

In a political sense, the de-stabilization of American labor fits the needs of progressives internationally, starting with the United Nations, which openly proposes a One World Order (Agenda 21) as an achievable goal.

From gun control, to economic policy, to marketing, the United Nations' One World Order (Agenda 21) systematically disassembles the United States, replacing it with a monetized labor pool that is mostly offshore. This puts the UN in a clear conflict of interest, owing its very existence to the country it now proposes to dismantle or at least assimilate.

THE IMPACT OF INTERNATIONAL EXPORTS AND MANUFACTURING

The United States has been moving significant portions of its economy to other countries. The question becomes "with what are we filling the void?" I would propose that the offsetting import into the U. S. is the standard of living of the country to which we exported the jobs or other economic values.

As NAFTA began, we saw many jobs go into Mexico. What we also saw, and continue to see, is a continuing influx of people from south of the border. Many of these immigrants are coming into the country illegally. At that point, the economic impact of the exports appears to have been double. We exported the jobs with the associated reduction in GDP , income and tax revenue. We also imported people who were unaccustomed to the American economy and standard of living. They ultimately work for less money and are more likely to be dependent on American government for their support.

Taken on a larger scale, the net effect would be to help flatten the economy of the world by making the working class more "even" around the globe.

This is admittedly the most conspiratorial part of this book. In all my research, I had trouble digesting the idea that a single entity would advocate for such a plan. I encourage you to research it yourself. I defy you to dismiss the idea as a simple conspiracy theory of the paranoid culture.

THE NEW WORLD ORDER (AGENDA 21)

Since its beginning, the United Nations has been engaged in a systematic move toward a single world government. This seems natural for a group with the title of "United Nations".

In 1992, the UN developed and voted on a program for "New World Order (Agenda 21)". [54]

From an article on Renewamerica.Com : "the plan…includes building six-story apartment complexes along these train lines, intended to relocate civilians away from their farms and ranches, which will no longer be approved for residential development. If you want to know what researchers have discovered about this effort, a simple Google will lead you to all you ever wanted to know."[55]

This effort is driven by the thought that a single world government could more effectively eliminate all the ills of the world. From tyranny, to dictatorship, to totalitarianism, the evils of man may be, in some cases, legislated away. In most cases, however, the United Nations forces would enforce a one world government rule. This effort simply mandates the behavior of all men, with force if necessary.

With this mandate in mind, it becomes clear that the establishment of a two class society (those in power - and those not) is the only

---

54 http://www.thirdworldtraveler.com/New_World_Order/NWO_ConspiracyOrReal%3F.html

55 http://www.renewamerica.com/columns/cobb/130219

possible solution.

With this solution in place, only a single government would exist. If there were individual governments, they would become subservient to the One World Government.

In that process, the United States becomes a hindrance to the effort. The concepts provided for in the United States Constitution simply do not fit in the New World Order or Agenda 21. The right to self determination, assumption of innocence, free market trade and personal responsibility get swallowed up in the concept of the need for authoritarian government and of a government that "takes care of" the citizens subject to that government.

Therefore, since its inception, the United Nations goal has been to infiltrate the United States and encourage the integration of America with other societies.

DEMOCRACY AS A PRODUCT

As the United States encouraged the United Nations to take on the role of world police, some in the country viewed the export of democracy as a product. Unfortunately, that plays into the hands of those in the United Nations who would have the United States hated for it's sometimes seemingly imperialist behavior.

The United States is the standard bearer for liberty, individual rights and free enterprise. Unfortunately, these concepts cannot exist in the utopian world of sameness. They cannot exist in a world where all decision making emanates from a single "ruler".

ISOLATIONISTS ARE UNREALISTIC

For those who accuse the United Nations of engaging in statism on a world wide scale, there is a fear that the "One World Government" theory will reduce the standards of freedom and liberty everywhere.

With The United States engaged in worldwide products and services, some say any effort to keep or bring manufacturing to America is an isolationist policy.

In 2013, Ron Paul and his son Rand spoke of the need to avoid imperialist behavior.

During that time period, even Newt Gingrich, an admitted neocon, suggested the policy of exporting democracy may have been flawed.

IS GLOBALIZATION THE FUTURE?

Globalization is the thought that there will be a single world government. Is this a realistic thought?

Bearing in mind this might be a goal of the United Nations, one should not be surprised that the United Nations has been actively engaged in the process of exporting manufacturing to countries other than the United States.

Combined with efforts of big money influence and the United States Government, one can see how the United States job market continues to be manipulated in an effort to flatten the playing field internationally. One can also see how this has encouraged the United States to fundamentally change the labor force.

SUMMARY

The United Nations contributed to commoditization by working relentlessly to flatten the world market. The commoditization of American workers fit with the UN view of a single world order. Since American workers lived, worked and spent in an economy not available to the rest of the world, it became necessary to eliminate the stability of the American middle class and the workers who gained stability from the free market American economy.

CONCLUSIONS

From the standpoint of the United States, the UN will only make commoditization worse as it continues to advocate for a New World Order mentality, fully blending all civilization into a single world government.

The best approach for the future would be to isolate the United Nations from U. S. government policy as much as possible. While its efforts have some merit and it deserves some level of input from the United States, the United Nations should not be able to direct United States policy on any issue; in particular, labor policies that impact the future of commoditization.

Chapter 10

The Wal-Mart Factor

It is difficult to tell if Wal-Mart has simply been in the right place at the right time, or it has been part of the circumstances that created the commoditization. It is certain that Wal-Mart has had a major impact on retail markets in the United States. It is just as certain retail stores such as Wal-Mart have been the beneficiaries of a commoditized labor force. From the uncertainty of high unemployment and low workforce participation rates to the demand to pay less to the movement of manufacturing to other countries, Wal-Mart and her peers has been a participant in the commoditization of America′s work force.

Wal-Mart is not alone. Some of the other big box stores have benefitted as well. Target, Sam's, Kmart, and even some of the small box stores such as Dollar General and Family Dollar have participated heavily in the commoditized retail environment.

I call this the Wal-Mart factor not to claim that Wal-Mart is in any way a bad company. I am not even going to say that Wal-Mart is bad for the United States. Whether Wal-Mart is "bad" is a conversation for another book or venue.

I do, however, believe there are many conditions in the Wal-Mart factor that have contributed to the commoditization of the American workforce. Wal-Mart is, after all, a commodities dealer.

It simply makes sense that it uses its successful approach to commodity sales in managing the commodities that are their workers.

In this analysis, I believe we can see the American Way has been dismissed. In the process of exporting jobs to other countries, we have effectively reduced the acceptable living standards in this country to something between US standards and the country to which we export the work. In the never ending quest for the lowest price, Wal-Mart has gambled that most people (or at least their demographic) will indeed do anything for money. And many of the population who shop there have made Wal-Mart's bet pay off.

Is Wal-Mart bad? I don't know. Are some of their business practices questionable? I will leave that up to you to decide. Please join me as I point out some of the business practices that make me wonder……

THE WAL-MART FACTOR

I know many people who have been employed in almost every position imaginable at a Wal-Mart store. Many of them have not had a pleasant experience in their career with the nation's largest employer.

While it is true that Wal-Mart offers plenty of opportunity to work, and even to grow one's career, the methods to gain that work are sometimes not very clear or consistent, and some would say not very fair.

I have heard stories of sudden changes in schedules,

responsibilities and shifts. I have seen Wal-Mart employees commit tremendous time and effort to benefit Wal-Mart, only to be left out of compensation, whether that compensation is financial, time or recognition of the total effort.

This is not to say that Wal-Mart has been unique in their approach. They have simply been the most efficient and effective at deploying this model. There are many very large corporations that have engaged in international manufacturing; exporting jobs, innovation, opportunity, and American cash permanently outside the purview of the U. S. government and the citizens of the United States. The need to save money without considering those savings' impact on the American job market exists in a number of areas in the U. S. economy.

It is difficult to tell which came first, commoditized labor or Wal-Mart. Wal-Mart's current slogan is "Spend less, Live Better". This implies that saving their customers money is their highest priority. One could say that this is Wal-Mart's way of encouraging greed on the part of their customers. The continued popularity and market domination of Wal-Mart implies the American citizen wants that option, although it may be that the customer is simply too busy to think about it. It also seems this approach encourages customers to choose low price over all other issues – security, peace, good family life, etc.

I again remind us that Wal-Mart may not be at fault here. They may just be very good at capitalizing on the transition occurring in American society. Wal-Mart cannot be faulted for simply riding the wave of social change.

When Wal-Mart began, it wanted to provide access to a variety of items by taking those items to the customer. At the time, malls across the United States were still fairly popular, but many people had to travel to up to 20 miles or more to get to them. Wal-Mart systematically placed their stores in closer proximity to the people living in rural areas. By placing many of those stores between the customers' homes and the mall, it was an easy sale to make.

The problem with that philosophy is that Wal-Mart wants all of the market in towns where they can obtain it. The consequence was that many of the smaller "mom and pop" grocery and hardware stores simply could not compete with Wal-Mart's pricing and deep pockets. This is known as the "scorched earth" philosophy.

This at least gave the impression of Wal-Mart as a company with a "slash and burn" approach to local communities. Where the smaller communities had their small tire stores, hardware stores, grocery stores, fix it shops and the like, Wal-Mart simply comes in to that market and eliminates them all.

In the next few sections of this chapter, we will talk about some of the market domination that has caused the Wal-Mart factor to be such a significant force in American society.

CONTROL (DOMINATE?) THE MARKET

Wal-Mart's approach to market domination was not always such a scorched earth approach. In the early years their stores were quite patriotic, displaying flags and "Made in America" symbols throughout the stores. Many of the lobbies had a large American flag in them and a "Made in The USA" logo below the flag. Sam Walton was very proud of this country. At least part of his motivation was the fact he sold American made goods.

As Wal-Mart and its market share grew (and Sam Walton passed away), there was a clear move to control the markets where its stores existed. Wal-Mart used fairly standard business practices in order to accomplish these controls. By providing access to most of the products Americans purchased much closer to home, it was quite natural that Americans would flock to the stores, possibly buying things they might have otherwise simply done without, or at least waited for. By providing access to these products at a cheaper price, and making price the single focus of retail, Wal-Mart ensured a high volume of sales for every store regardless of its location. There is a joke that says Wal-Mart knows what you will be buying before you walk into their stores. There is something admirable as well as creepy about a retailer with that much power and knowledge.

In more recent history, Wal-Mart has become a market dominating machine. They have a "just in time" delivery process and a market presence that is most definitely scorched earth. Their ability to analyze local markets and control every individual aspect of the market at each individual store means Wal-Mart can lean the product cycle down to the tiniest of cost. By establishing a presence in the center of every town and then dictating the retail environment, Wal-Mart can crush the small mom and pop stores

wherever they are present.
This approach is used by many other retail companies, but Wal-Mart owns the majority of that space. The ability to provide so many products so regularly and at such a cheap price is quite impressive. The innovations they bring to retail are leading not just Wal-Mart but many other retailers to efficiencies not possible before these times.
Market control has, however, come at a price to the U. S. citizen, economy, tax base and manufacturing base. The mantra of "Save Money. Live Better" needs to have a disclaimer - "regardless of what it does to your career, your family, or your country". With a focus on their market, and by having a presence in almost every market in the country, Wal-Mart has dominated retail. Just look at the mall you used to go to regularly. When is the last time you went to the mall? When is the last time you went to Wal-Mart? Recently I drove around the neighborhood where my employer is located looking for a grocery store. The Wal-Mart sits where a small mall was located for many years. The neighborhood was, at one time, the center of a large middle class lifestyle for thousands of people living on the south side of Nashville.
Today, there is only one choice for groceries. Kroger is gone, as is the Kmart, which recently closed after over fifty years in that location. A large compliment of Hispanics lives in the neighborhood, and there are a few specialty stores for groceries. But if I want to buy lunch and breakfast items or snacks, I have to bring them with me from home as Wal-Mart is my only choice –

and I avoid going there.

CONTROL MANUFACTURING

Another approach of retailers is to dictate who manufactures a product by dictating price. For years, there has been a process of RFQ or RFP (Request for Quote or Request for Process) that determined the cost of producing an item. This cost was then the basis of the retail price of an item. Most retailers used cost plus as their foundation for a retail price. In that process, retail profit was a more fixed number. This model was not just the foundation of profit on a product; it was also what allowed manufacturing to account for the cost of making a product using U. S. labor.

Over the course of its existence, Wal-Mart has changed the manufacturing process. Given its extremely large sales numbers, Wal-Mart now has the option to dictate the price. This has been a change in approach for manufacturing and others wanting access to American markets. It is also symptomatic of a problem that comes as a single retail outlet gains what is arguably a monopoly on a large portion of any retail market. The retail outlet begins to dictate what is available, at what quality and with what features. By virtue of this type of dictation of retail price, they now are dictating how a product is manufactured, where it is manufactured, who manufactures it and how it arrives at their stores.

By dictating the cost of a product, Wal-Mart changes the game for everyone in the retail business. For Wal-Mart, whose model this is, it fits their just in time approach and the limited stocking of inventory. It guarantees volume of product for distribution. It also applies enormous pressure on other retailers to sell products for the same low price – regardless of whether they can purchase the item below that price, if at all. As we have seen, some have been able to keep up. However, many have not. In the game of retail, Wal-Mart has the advantage. It controls the manufacturing process, because it controls the sales process.

If America intended to stay in manufacturing, this could have been a win-win solution. Unfortunately, it has forced America to abandon manufacturing and shift to a service economy. The commoditization of Wal-Mart workers has continued as we lose the demand for skilled manufacturing labor.

CONTROL THE WORKFORCE

Wal-Mart has worked quite hard to avoid unionization of its work force. It also works aggressively at dictating compensation and worker engagement. This causes Wal-Mart to have what might be considered as an unfair competitive advantage because they are not negotiating with employees using the same standards as their competition.

I am sure many will applaud this management style, but it is short sighted - and contributes heavily to the commoditization of the work force in the U. S. They also heavily dictate the hourly rate paid for employees' time. I will admit Wal-Mart is not alone in this effort, but they are the largest employer in The United States[56], so other businesses follow the Wal-Mart example. Should Wal-Mart control the hourly rate? Absolutely. Should the workers have input into the hourly rate? In a free market economy, one would think so. With commoditization of the work force, that rate may be determined by factors other than the market, particularly if Wal-Mart wants it that way.

Another Wal-Mart tactic is to control the number of hours for which employees are paid. By controlling the number of hours an employee is engaged, Wal-Mart determines which employees qualify for full time status. Wal-Mart determines the definition of full time status. In some cases, retailers have redefined the status known as fulltime from 40 to 32 hours per week. By controlling the number of hours, employees are also limited in their access to benefit programs Wal-Mart pays for, converting these benefits so they come from government (taxpayer funded) benefit programs. In this way, some argue Wal-Mart is receiving "corporate welfare" in terms of benefits they do not have to pay for provided they suppress their employees' income.

CONTROL THE GOVERNMENT

Wal-Mart is the largest private company in American retail. With just over two million employees, Wal-Mart demands, and receives, beneficial treatment in a wide variety of places in the American economy.

---

[56] http://en.wikipedia.org/wiki/Walmart

The leviathan, behemoth is the largest private employer in the U. S. It holds approximately 63% of the retail market in America. Wal-Mart is in the position to demand and receive a variety of tax benefits just by virtue of giving the appearance it provides jobs in the communities they "invade". To politicians, and maybe some citizens, this may look like a good idea.

The government engages in multiple crony capitalist and socialist deals with Wal-Mart as a social engineering experiment. Wal-Mart is the beneficiary of corporate welfare as it continues to pay substandard wages and while granting insufficient hours to bring the employee above an income level qualifying them for government assistance. In this way, Wal-Mart receives a government funded stipend for every employee they hire and pay. In the case of low and mid level managers, this perception of being the largest employer gives Wal-Mart the benefit of new employees wanting to climb the corporate ladder at Wal-Mart, even if that means “paying their dues”.

CONTROL LABOR

As we have pointed out, Wal-Mart has not been a friend of organized labor. Stories abound of employees attempting to organize, and the lengths Wal-Mart has been willing to go to in order to keep those organizing efforts from being successful.

This is an understandable approach for the largest private employer in the United States. Labor costs are significant. To a high margin, low profit, business every penny has the chance of having a large impact on profits.

Wal-Mart's approach to labor has been three tiered:

1) Control full time opportunities

Wal-Mart severely restricts access to full time employment for the resources available to their stores.

2) Control part time opportunities

Wal-Mart has shown a tendency to restrict access to part time employment for resources by narrowing the available hours, preferably below 28 hours each week.

3) Control salaries, hourly labor rates and benefit packages.

Salary and hourly rates are contained to some of the lowest in any industry, not just retail. Hourly employees are subject to extremely low rates as well as demands of working beyond their scheduled time, sometimes requesting these employees work off the clock. In addition, benefit packages are somewhat depressed and employees absorb the majority of the costs.

Along with this approach, Wal-Mart continues to engage in systematically understaffing its operations. In 2014, Wal-Mart experienced another consequence of this understaffing when it announced the un-stocked shelves in Wal-Mart stores were impacting profitability in some stores.[57][58]

---

[57] http://www.bloomberg.com/news/2013-03-26/customers-flee-wal-mart-empty-shelves-for-target-costco.html

[58] http://www.nytimes.com/2013/04/04/business/walmart-strains-to-keep-grocery-aisles-stocked.html?pagewanted=all&_r=0

THE HIGH COST OF LOW PRICE

This documentary film is a controversial movie written about Wal-Mart. It is written with the help of former employees at a large number of Wal-Mart stores. It is a revealing story worth watching, outlining the issues with the domination of Wal-Mart in the retail space. In recent years, it has become difficult to find. Do what you can to find it. The film does give the viewer a different perspective.

BUY AMERICAN?

While Wal-Mart had its start in selling products manufactured in the U. S. , that approach diminished as the banking, government and financial sectors began their efforts to internationalize the United States. We discuss those situations elsewhere in this book.

As Wal-Mart became more dependent on foreign manufacturing, and as government and financial entities were deliberately moving manufacturing away from the United States, Wal-Mart's advocacy for American goods diminished. Arguing that the cost of labor was too high and that regulation was too stringent, "off shoring" retail made a decent case for sourcing of goods outside the United States. When Sam Walton was alive and growing the Wal-Mart franchise, a person walking into one of his stores would immediately encounter a large American flag on the wall and the words "Made In The USA" painted on the wall. There were many American made products in the stores - many of them made near the stores where they were sold.

Once Mr. Walton passed away, the "Buy American" program was gone. [59]

RE-SHORING

Since the 1980's, America has been shipping jobs "offshore". The discussions on this subject have a wide and varied range. Much like the discussions about protectionism, empirical data for either case is highly subject to the viewpoint of the person interpreting the data. Very few cases exist that prove a case either way.

In 2010 and beyond, the move has been made not out of patriotism, but out of economics. Companies re-shoring operations in a number of areas have discovered the costs of shipping, risks of inventory and other classic issues offset any perceived savings that have been realized.

They have also discovered that Americans need jobs and are willing to work for far less compensation than previously offered.

MIKE ROWE AND WAL-MART'S "BUY AMERICAN" PROGRAM

In January 2014, Wal-Mart hired Mike Rowe, a popular actor and spokesman, to introduce their new "Buy American" program. The program met with mixed reviews as Mike tried to talk about all of the American manufacturing jobs Wal-Mart intended to "create".

---

[59] http://www.huffingtonpost.com/stacy-mitchell/walmart-buy-america_b_3795011.html

60

The company laid claim to fifty billion dollars in new manufacturing in the United States.[61] Using an old political trick, rather than say this was five billion per year; they chose to say it was fifty billion dollars over ten years.[62]

This amount of manufacturing is a mere 1.5 % of total annual sales for Wal-Mart.

THE INTERNET

The Internet has also been an influence in the Wal-Mart factor. Many people now spend time shopping for items on line rather than in a store. Wal-Mart has managed to compete in this market by implementing several innovative programs. The ability to stand up high performance websites makes Wal-Marts sites very competitive. The pricing is always very competitive and the site to store model allows Wal-Mart to take advantage of its distribution network to help offset shipping charges.

The federal and state governments got involved by injecting the sales tax into the mix. While this is still an ongoing legislative

---

60 http://www.salon.com/2014/03/07/walmarts_newest_big_lie_another_misleading_ad_campaign_from_a_job_killing_behemoth/

61 http://www.today.com/money/testing-wal-marts-made-usa-campaign-2D11678842

62 http://news.walmart.com/executive-viewpoints/inside-walmarts-50-billion-buy-american-campaign

battle, the collection of individual state taxes adds a level of complexity to the transaction. It also reduces the impact of a decision based on not having to pay the tax.

ELIMINATE COMPETITION

The existence of companies operating in the extreme discount space has contributed to the elimination of many companies which, at one time, provided many of the household items Americans depended on. Combined with their building themselves into the customer's lives, companies like Sears, J.C. Penney and Montgomery Ward co-existed in a retail space for a very long time. One could argue that Wal-Mart helped reduce the number of shopping malls and with them many of the large retail chains that occupied those malls.

Companies like Wal-Mart may not have originally decided to eliminate their competition, but it has been a great help to their market footprint. As I have said, Wal-Mart has over 11000 stores internationally. They employ almost 2.2 million people internationally, with 1.4 million people employed in the United States[63]. They were responsible for 3% of the GDP in retail sales in 2012.[64] One of every four dollars spent in America on groceries is spent at Wal-Mart.[65]

---

[63] http://stock.walmart.com/financial-reporting/unit-counts-square-footage/

[64] https://get.com/economy/2011/07/18/walmart-the-most-successful-retailer-in-history/

[65] http://www.businessinsider.com/crazy-facts-about-walmart-2012-11?op=1

Wal-Mart's entire existence appears to have been to eliminate competition, one of the engines of capitalist society and free markets.

The consequence of running your competition out of town is that you no longer have any competition. Many successful retail companies have realized the value and importance of having competitors around any business.

Competition is known to be good for all business. But what happens when there is no competition? Monopolization can bring disastrous results as price, quality and availability become controlled by a single entity. Sure, it's great to save money, but what happens when all the competition is gone and the monopolized retailer decides to simply raise the price? What happens if that retailer decides you don't need another TV? Where will you buy it then?

SAVE MONEY, LIVE BETTER?

When your approach follows this philosophy, whose money are you saving? There has been a wealth of entrants into the extreme low margin, high volume retail business. Extreme low prices have indeed allowed some people to at least have the illusion that lower prices will allow us to live better.

The tendency of people to want to purchase items for less is a reference to a natural phenomenon. However, many do not consider the true cost of lower prices. Reduced quality, questionable products and the need to have it now have driven people to justify paying lower and lower prices for products without any consideration for where the product comes from, who is making the product, or what it does to support the nation.

Access to markets outside this country combine with depressed economies in those countries to give the impression that saving money comes without consequence either in lifestyle, foreign economies or the impact on the citizens of the foreign countries who are producing these products. I refer us again to the thousands of people killed in other countries while producing the products on which we are saving money.

When we stop to consider the American citizens who are largely unable to manage their personal budgets and who have a hunger for (possibly an addiction) to instant gratification, we are left with a perception that a better life can be bought with material possessions. While this might be true from the standpoint of a person looking for access to basic possessions such as food, clothing or medicine, it is doubtful that many of the items being purchased actually contribute to the living of a better life.

IT ISN'T ALL WAL-MART'S FAULT

The Wal-Mart Factor is not in the book to say that Wal-Mart is an evil enterprise bent on world domination. Certainly, Wal-Mart serves a purpose in many communities.

The Wal-Mart Factor may be secondary to the other items mentioned in this book. The Wal-Mart factor absolutely applies to other retailers. Target, Kmart and many other retailers are chasing the success of Wal-Mart and following some of the same tactics I mention in this chapter.

Commoditization of everything that exists is certainly underway in America, possibly in the world. Wal-Mart may have simply been in the right place at the right time. There are certainly people who have opposed the Wal-Mart factor and have openly chosen not to shop in a Wal-Mart. There are things Wal-Mart does not sell (appliances are one example).

The story of Sam Walton and his enterprise is a uniquely American story of a person who saw a need and filled it. This is a story of innovation that could only have occurred in The United States. Mr. Walton dreamed of success and discovered it in the corporation he founded. It became more successful than he could imagine and it did that because of free enterprise. I believe this success could only have happened in America.

There are lessons in the Wal-Mart Factor, and there are clues for the coming generations of this country. It is still possible Wal-Mart might decide to help this country by fostering American production of the goods sold in its stores, at least the items sold in the United States. I am convinced Wal-Mart's customer base would be enlarged by developing a policy of selling uniquely American products, even if they cost up to 20% more. I believe Wal-Mart customers who are American citizens are prepared to take their money elsewhere, even with some inconvenience, in order to gain access to products that are “Made in The USA”.

Whether they would be uniquely sold or would be sold right next to the less expensive products, I believe Wal-Mart holds the keys to that plan, and could help bring back competitors such as Kmart, Sears, Penney's and others as they openly embrace American made products. Only time will tell.

GREED

At what point does the protection of a corporation's profits become greed? I wonder why no one sees the export of jobs, then the re-import of the products, as treasonous, if that practice destabilizes the country?

In the process of taxation and regulation, who is to say if the tax code is written to benefit the retailer, thereby making it easy for Wal-Mart to send jobs elsewhere?

Wal-Mart's CEO was paid over twenty five million dollars in 2014.[66] This is more in an hour than the average Wal-Mart employee makes in a year.[67]

Whether this is capitalism and free enterprise or greed is a discussion for another time. In the meantime, I encourage you to consider the question and try to come up with an answer.

CONSUMERS

Consumers have contributed to the Wal-Mart factor as well. When do we consider the full impact of low price? What has happened to the idea that we contribute to our community when we make our

---

[66] http://www.arkansasbusiness.com/article/98329/wal-mart-ceo-doug-mcmillon-earned-256-million-last-year

[67] http://abcnews.go.com/Business/walmart-ceo-pay-hour-workers-year/story?id=11067470

purchases locally? Has the consumer been convinced that price is the only measure and that where the item comes from no longer has any bearing on the purchasing decision? Is the consumer prepared to pay more for locally produced products? It appears they might, at least in the case of food.[68] But when it comes to manufactured articles that may not be the case. Wal-Mart is selling what the consumer wants. That is definitely free enterprise and a uniquely capitalist concept.

REDUCTION OF MALLS

Either Wal-Mart's timing was very good, or customers were ready for a change in the type of shopping experience they were having. Whichever it was, Wal-Mart benefitted from this massive change in demographics.

It appears the timing was a bit of a perfect storm. Customers were looking for a new experience. Malls had become a bit different and were sometimes not easy to go shopping. The Internet was invading the retail space, removing sales taxes from many goods. Wal-Mart came along with their "cheaper is better" model just in time to take advantage of the timing of these events.

Malls didn't have a chance from there. Some malls have survived by making the experience as much about entertainment as it is about shopping. Others survived because of their middle to upper class demographic. Those that did not survive crashed hard, taking

---

[68] http://www.foodnavigator.com/Science-Nutrition/Consumers-will-pay-more-for-local-foods-Study

neighborhoods with them as they fundamentally changed the surrounding economies.

SUMMARY

Wal-Mart has taken advantage of timing. Some would say they have taken unfair advantage. In every aspect of their business model, they have commoditized the products, facilities and human resources.

Of course, they have every right to do what they have done. Consumers have chosen to make them the largest retailer in history. Have they enjoyed an unfair advantage from government? Have they benefitted from the monopoly they have rolled across the country? Do they benefit from the commoditization of the American worker? You decide.

CONCLUSIONS

The Wal-Mart factor is prevalent throughout the United States. Whether Wal-Mart caused this or is simply taking advantage of the situation is up for discussion. As the American worker is commoditized and as the middle class disappears, Wal-Mart is a force that can ensure that consumers can afford the item they consume. Is this a sustainable model? I don't think so.

Chapter 11

The Conventional Job

The United States labor market has a long history of providing very diverse opportunities for a very large segment of the population. Let's take a look at what that conventional labor force might have looked like.

THE LABOR DRIVEN WORKFORCE

When I was growing up, I worked many different jobs; first as a paper boy. This is one of those jobs that has fallen victim to the changes in our society as many of us have shifted from dependence on print media to electronic and internet based media. There is still a lot to be said for the tactile experience that was being a paper boy. For me, there is still a lot to be said for the tactile experience that is reading the paper, or a book.

I was around 13 or 14 years old when we began those paper routes. Since my dad was transferred from Tennessee to Arkansas as part of his Air Force assignment, we lived on base housing at Little Rock Air Force Base. My brother and I "threw" papers every day, with Sunday consuming mass amounts of time for us because the Sunday papers were so much larger than the daily paper. We also had many more subscribers to the paper on Sunday. We always had nicer bicycles and the best of any tools we needed to get the work done. For instance, while most carriers had pliers to cut the papers loose (yes - they were bound with wire), we had a little ring with slots in it that fit in our pocket.

We grew that business pretty well, although I don't really remember thinking of it as a business. I don't remember the quantities of papers sold or delivered, but it was a very large number. The count was so big that we could afford to buy a car to lug the papers around on cold or rainy days. This would be the beginning of a life "working" for a living and was really my first exposure to a labor driven workforce. Of course, the success of this business depended on the free labor of mom and dad to drive the car.

In considering this situation, I am left to reflect on two things: First, my Dad had a military work ethic. My mother had a farm girl work ethic. As a result, from my first memory, work was a part of our daily lives. My parents did a great job of exposing us to work in the conventional sense. Hard work was simply a part of our lives and Dad particularly pointed out how an ability and willingness to work should be a high priority.

The second is a more personal situation. Nonetheless it is what became an overriding part of my life for many years. While we had a very strong work ethic and were raised not to fear work, our parents did very little to teach us what has become known as "work/life balance". Work became our only motivator as everything was subject to work life. This is what I now call the "Brute Force Methodology". In a life filled with pounding square pegs into round holes, there is no way to achieve fulfillment. If we do not decide to establish the boundaries required to have a fulfilling life, something will break. In many cases, this is another unsustainable model. If nothing else, as we age, we simply cannot possibly continue to put that much effort into our endeavors.

Along with that concept came a lack of recognition for the Sabbath. I will not spend much time talking about it, my other books do that, but I am certain the lack of establishing limits on work time, and for me, particularly Sunday, followed me through my career. Sunday was just another day, and another day to work. This is simply not a sustainable way to live. Whether you are religious or not, God's mandate to take a day off may be applied in each of our lives. A day of rest is simply a part of managing our lives.

I mention these things because I know far too many people who have made their living entirely by brute force. While it is an honorable character trait, it is a terribly short sited viewpoint that fails to recognize the futility of the effort and of the inevitability that pure labor will not always be an abundant resource for many of us.

A strong work ethic is critical to the success of a nation. More than any other motivation, including the support of our families, that ethic ensures we go to work each day simply because we should. The willingness to work, and to work hard, at whatever we choose to do is an indicator of a willingness to get things done. There is a need for a person to have personal initiative and not waste away sitting idly by waiting for some other force to impact our efforts. For a century or more, this labor driven workforce has been the primary contributor to our flourishing nation. Since the advent of production line manufacturing, the labor force in the United States had a challenge. Their admirable calling was to be the best, fastest and most innovative force in the world. This workforce met every challenge handed to it, and did so with remarkable quality as well. Despite those who would say American products are/were sub-standard, Americans were always on the leading edge of product development and deployment. As a purely labor driven workforce, our country used that labor to establish itself as a highly productive group. We managed to get over the concept of "sweat shops" and of forced labor. We used the labor driven work force to improve people's lives and standard of living as well.

SUMMARY

The conventional U.S. job was what we sometimes referred to as a career. For generations, Americans aspired to achieve the American Dream. This aspiration often included a job of some sort and often included a career at "the plant" or some other manufacturing facility.

Some of these people became plumbers, carpenters, auto mechanics, truck drivers or other trades. In many cases, those trades were represented by unions.

Where they weren't represented, they were the beneficiaries of work force policies influenced by union negotiations or contracts.

Employers offered salaries and benefit packages that supported the middle class. Some of these jobs were often labor intensive, requiring intense physical demands. Even though it was sometimes intense, the conventional job produced the stability of a middle class that became the foundation of the entire American work force.

CONCLUSIONS

There is not much that may be done to return us to this style of work force. There are many lessons that may be examined in developing the new commoditized work force that might help stabilize or re-establish the middle class. The conventional job that allowed a large segment of the United States to become employed, mature in their profession or trade, aspire for retirement and then retire has been replaced with a commoditized society that offers almost none of the securities of the conventional job.

Chapter 12

The Role of Money

When I was growing up, money was a mysterious thing to me. In the 1960's we were part of the "middle class". With a house, one or two cars and living paycheck to paycheck, we simply had what we needed, and very little extra. I was beginning to be aware of friends, neighbors and acquaintances that seemed to have their finances in order, but I had not been exposed to financial management in a proactive sense. It all just seemed to happen automatically.

In those times, societal greed had not yet set in. It was there, but the middle class had not yet gotten "the bug". It seemed enough that we lived by the mantra, "An honest day's work for an honest day's pay."

As an Air Force brat, I was used to moving a lot. We rarely owned our home because we lived in base housing a lot. Once we did buy a house, it had a sizeable mortgage. Even that was presented to us as a normal situation; "everyone" lived that way. Living as a leveraged society would be an easy change to make once that became more prevalent in the 1980's and beyond. It was simply assumed everyone would have a long term mortgage on their house. As long as a person had a "job for life", this obligation did not seem so bad.

I mention this because part of the risk of commoditization is many of us find ourselves with the home mortgage obligation, but without the "job for life". Today, a fully leveraged home is a "normal" way to live for many Americans. This fully leveraged lifestyle contributes to the reactionary model, "forcing" us to work harder, stay in a job we do not care for, or make less ethical decisions as we go about our daily roles of generating enough money to pay the bills. Certainly, the "requirement" for both parents to be out of the home is contributing to a less family-centric nation, and a mortgage drives one of the parents away from parenthood.

Employers know this about the working class. There are plenty of examples of a worker who is less productive and efficient than they might be if they had the freedom to do what they love as opposed to doing what they have to do. The employer is more than willing to allow the employee to back themselves into a corner with high debt or with a more expensive lifestyle than they can afford. Thus, a sort of voluntary servitude is put in place. Once the debt is incurred and the worker is at his limit, they are on the treadmill, with no way off. Purely reactive, they become "trapped" in their job and lifestyle. At one time, companies would factor in the ineffective, inefficient employees and would factor in the cost of keeping them around, assigning them to perform easy or general tasks. Today, you find many of these positions are the first to be commoditized. Particularly if those workers are in the service trades, those with no or limited direct revenue producing skills may never find meaningful work.

The financial industry knows this, benefitting from the reactive nature of those making up the working class. Living in a fully leveraged home, driving leveraged cars and spending money not yet earned costs the working class more than just financially. It costs the working class in terms of security, safety and even serenity. Banks and financial industries are the beneficiaries of that behavior financially. For conventional financial entities, they make their revenue via conventional means. The more leveraged the worker becomes, or the less careful the worker is about their earnings, the more they "need" the services of the "bottom dwellers" of the financial industry. Payday advance and title loan companies begin to "service" those who are deemed unworthy for service by conventional lenders. These predatory lenders profit with interest rates of four hundred to six hundred percent, which can only be classified as usury.

The education industry also plays its part in the manipulation of labor with money. Money causes workers to perceive that more education will ensure (almost guarantee) a person will make more money. In many cases it will, but money by itself may not automatically lead to the life many workers perceive.

Finally, government knows of the impact of money on the labor force. For all the reasons previously stated, money motivates people. The danger in government's approach is that motivation may not be for the good of the country, but for the good of the government (or the enlargement of government programs). The government uses money in a social experiment to fundamentally change the landscape of the United States. In my parent's generation, my mother was a homemaker, choosing to stay home to raise her family and ensure we had a very comfortable and fulfilling life. I apologize if this concept is offensive to those who might view a homemaker as somehow less than a person who goes to work each day. But look at the impact of the social experiment of the two income family. In tax base alone, this self serving approach by the government has suited it very well.

This has been an ongoing theme in the book. I have tried to make it less sinister and more factual, but it will feel as if there is a giant conspiracy working against the American citizen. I worked to have it not so, but there is clearly something in the American culture that has changed about how people support their families. Being commoditized is great for those who have skills that are in demand, but if you find yourself commoditized without skills, finding employment in anything other than menial labor is an elusive endeavor. When I look for a root cause, I see many manipulations occurring over the last 50 years that have served to place the interests of bankers, educators, and government over the needs of the American citizen.

In the last few chapters, I attempted to discuss the root cause of the situation in which we find ourselves as a country today. The intellectuals will blow me off as a novice. The working class may deem the book boring as they do with many things (like voting?) that have a major impact on their futures. Those of us stuck on the conveyor belt of life will simply not be able to stay awake long enough to read it all.

This would be a good place to mention a book that gives a new perspective to our existence. Titled "It's OK to Leave the Plantation", this book tells the story of the American slave, the social engineering in that effort and of the possibility that Americans, particularly black Americans, never really left slavery, they simply continued to be slaves in a different system.

For those who have made good financial decisions all their lives, have plenty of savings and retirement, or may have their home paid for by around 50 years of age, much of this book will simply make little sense, and may not matter. Their perspective is one of elitism or lack of empathy for those struggling because of financial status. The excuse of the person being victim to poor choice will somehow relieve a person from needing empathy? There can be no question financial status is a major driving factor determining why people find themselves struggling as they do, particularly now that they have been commoditized.

I also hope some of the book brings an opportunity for us to face the truth about where we are as a country. Money has been an enormous motivator for greed, terrorism, hate and abuse in America. Trust and honesty have suffered. Friendships and relationships have been destroyed. Sadly, people who at one time had been thought of as solid, truthful and trustworthy continue to make financial choices that may destroy them, and often others with whom they come in contact.

PERSONAL CREDIT

I believe during the conventional phase of the country, credit was more rare, and used for much smaller ventures. The percentage of people who owned their homes outright has remained fairly steady. This condition was a safer one in that a person felt their home was the source of peace and that they always had a place to stay. However, for those with mortgages, equity as a share of total household real estate began declining in the mid-1980s.[69] This trend towards less equity in more recent times has contributed to the commoditization of American labor as the highly leveraged lifestyle forces workers to remain in the market in order to pay off their homes.

Today, I am left to conclude that consumer credit has become far too prevalent in America, leading to some of the issues we have experienced.

Certainly, in previous times, people were more content to make do with what they had and to "suffer" a bit in anticipation of the life they were pursuing. If credit was used, it was used sparingly and certainly not for comfort items in most cases. As the old saying goes, "Use it up, wear it out, make it do, or do without". Since the late 1990s, not many people are doing without in the sense that this phrase implies.

Later in my teenage years, my parents ran a “Mom and Pop” store

---

[69] http://www.heritage.org/research/reports/2014/06/why-is-federal-housing-policy-fixated-on-30-year-fixed-rate-mortgages

where they "carried" balances for people on house accounts. Just small accounts, these were used to get people by from time to time. Milk, eggs, bread, a little gas every now and then. This is the first place I remember being aware of all of the different types of interest; none, simple and compound interest was a concept I understood, but I rarely thought about, otherwise controlled, or tried to negotiate the terms.

As credit flowed more freely, people began to elevate their lifestyles, often with credit. Unlike paying with cash, where the choice to live a better lifestyle is paid for at the point of purchase, paying with credit delayed the costs without delaying the gratification. Unfortunately, when elevating one's lifestyle on credit, the negative impact to the purchaser/borrower is a much more destabilizing factor. The stress of making monthly or weekly payments becomes a motivator for producing "more", whatever more means at the time (it is not always money). In addition, the cost of the credit begins to gnaw away at the income itself, a slippery slope that demands a constant increase in revenue to the family.

In another example, when a person has a mortgage on their primary residence, their need for full-time employment will cause many of them to consider behavior not otherwise considered. When it comes time to make a decision whether to tell the truth, or tell a little white lie, a person whose livelihood depends on that paycheck may be more prone to tell a story. As a result, the ability of the employer to trust their employees becomes shaded by the ethical strength of the work force. Once the employer establishes that some margin of deception exists in a full-time employee, we see one more justification for a commoditized work force.

In addition, the manipulation of finances by those providing the financing has become more onerous over time. There is a ridiculous thing in financial circles known as an amortization table. This is a product of something called the rule of seventy eights, a process where the interest is "front loaded" on loan payments. This means the borrower pays the lender the cost of the financing in advance of paying anything on the item purchased. In the case of a home, unless the loan is paid off for the term of the loan, the effective interest rate when compared to simple interest is actually considerably more than the interest rate stated on the loan.

Personal credit used for instant gratification can be an evil concept; it continues to ruin people's lives. So why do it? Because financial interests make money at it. Why does the government condone it? Because the financial and government people benefit from this usurious behavior.

Government policies regarding home ownership and mortgages have led the U. S. to a unique situation. According to The American Enterprise Institute “The United States is the only developed country with a significant role in housing policy.” They further state “In 1989, for example, only 1 in 230 homebuyers made a down payment of 3 percent or less; by 2007, it was 1 in 3. Meanwhile, average home equity plunged from 45 percent to 7 percent." [70]

SUMMARY

Financial influences in the United States, and throughout the world, have appeared to advocate for a severe reduction in the standards of business. They also appear to have been actively engaged in diminishing the role of labor in determining their own fate. Finally, financial players have engaged in social engineering experiments with governments in exchange for profit, much of it personal, to a few politicians and financiers.

United States government involvement in finance and in the housing market in general, have contributed to the commoditization of the workforce as they manipulated home ownership and mortgage behaviors.

CONCLUSIONS

Commoditization of labor has cheapened everything. The key is for financial markets to realize the value labor brings to the relationship. As labor is commoditized, the working class will begin to realize they need to pay much more attention to finance. Hopefully, this will lead to more conservative financial behavior on the part of the commoditized worker. A willingness to wait for larger purchases or even items one cannot afford will develop as the commoditized worker uses more caution financially.

---

[70] http://www.aei.org/outlook/economics/financial-services/housing-finance/free-fall-how-government-policies-brought-down-the-housing-market/

Chapter 13

The Commoditized Job

The commoditized job has been the product of all of the efforts of the entities discussed in previous chapters. I believe you can see the impact each one has individually. The cumulative impact has been a wholesale change in the American labor market.

WHAT DO YOU "DO" FOR A LIVING?

There was a time when Americans were tradesmen. Professionals at whatever they did, they went through their lives climbing "the hill" in an effort to get to the top, where they then waited to retire as they mentored others in their trade.

Tradesmen came in many shapes and disciplines. They were not just men. Women were fully engaged in almost every trade or profession possible. This country was full of innovative and intuitive individuals who were adept at multiple trades. They were carpenters, mechanics, painters, steelworkers, electricians, iron workers, truckers, teachers, government workers and many others in union jobs that were lifelong careers.

There were just as many tradesmen in these and other areas who were not unionized, but who did the work necessary to keep this country moving. Car mechanics, carpenters, painters, janitors, salesmen and women, and many other people worked their trades by providing services and manufactured goods necessary to the forward movement of a free nation.

In addition, there were full-time parents. Unlike the family of today, many parents chose to stay home and take care of raising their children. No small task, these were selfless people. Mostly women, they "sacrificed" their lives in the ultimate role - that of raising children, and sometimes raising husbands. An old saying says, “Behind every successful man stands a woman” - indeed.

In previous times, everyone knew what they "did" for a living, many often choosing that role early and sticking with it, providing the accuracy and efficiency that could only come from knowing one's trade. In many small towns across America, teenagers dreamed of going to work at “the plant” because that meant their lives would be permanently changed for the better. The security and certainty that came from those jobs ensured the middle class would be protected.

COMMODITIZED

Now, workers have become commodities. Reduced to always selling themselves to the next customer, they are stuck in mediocrity. No longer are the days when a person has a profession. Rather, the profession has them; temporarily. Mean and hateful managers, directors and corporate officers have diminished the contribution of the fully seasoned professional.

Even someone in a menial task, such as janitor, once had extreme value. I remember with fondness the service workers I have met who could be counted on to provide their service with exactness, precision and professionalism. Now, even those workers have been commoditized.

It is unclear what a career is made of. It is entirely a mystery what the future might contain. What we have today is a much diminished workforce as a result. As a result, many do not know what they contribute to in the workforce. Many have no idea what their future looks like because what they contribute is just a simple, often temporary, commoditized service.

WHAT IS A COMMODITIZED WORKER?

A commodity is defined as

1) A raw material or primary agricultural product that can be bought and sold, such as copper or coffee.

2) A useful or valuable thing, such as water or time.[71]

Please note the rather secondary reference to time as being a commodity. This is one of the main engines for making commodities of us all. As the American workforce becomes more commoditized, we sell the intangible commodity known as time. This time has value, negotiable value, and needs to be recognized in the terms of any other commodity.

You will see references in many of my books to a bishop once telling me "You can always make more money, but you can never make more time". This tells us that the need for us to protect our limited time and to exact maximum benefit from its sale is

[71] https://www.google.com/?gws_rd=ssl#q=definition+of+commodity

paramount. With that in mind, many of us have become commodities traders, offering pure services in a sort of commodity traders market. Whether the commodity is time, knowledge or a warm body is often not clear until after we are “hired”.

As we examine our time from the standpoint of commoditization, we see very rapidly that our time is subject to the laws of supply and demand. Consequently, as we drill down into what makes that time valuable as a commodity, we see using that time to provide services is also something we need to understand fully in order to provide a price for it. As workers used to being paid either an hourly or salary compensation package, a commoditized pricing will be a new realm for us.

This commoditization requires us to be ready to negotiate based on what we can do, how well we can do it, and how much the client wants us to do the work. The commodity has a fluctuating price and value as a result.

ARE YOU THE COMMODITY?

Being a human commodity can sometimes be a bit demeaning. You will have experiences that will make you wonder if you are comfortable with the concept of your being a commodity. You will need to ponder and answer the question; "Am I a commodity?"

As we analyze the condition that is commoditization, we discover that the human being may not be the commodity exactly. Rather, the human's talents are the commodity and the human being is simply the method of delivery. Remember one of my sayings;

"You are not paying me to turn screws, you are paying me to know which screw to turn". Value comes from the knowledge we apply to our work.

That might only make the experience worse for you. It does take a different mindset to become a commoditized person. As a consultant, it will be necessary for you to change yourself, adjusting your thinking to the implied disposability of your skills and of your career, if "career" is the right term.

Many who have been in the contracting/consulting business have seen the value in surrendering to the experience and simply selling to the highest bidder.

Others have tried to find a middle ground, allowing them to provide the service while still maintaining a level of dignity as they lean toward the consulting side of things.

Some have been commoditized against their will. For instance, we have talked about Wal-Mart and their treatment of labor. Some people in the retail space have found themselves commoditized by having their full time jobs with benefits reduced to part time jobs with no benefits.

In all these cases, the sooner one realizes he/she is commoditized, the sooner one can define the "new paradigm" under which they work and define what will be needed to survive in that space. In many cases, this new situation requires active engagement of the commoditized worker in order to have that worker assess their part and make a well informed decision about what kind of commodity they intend to be.

Realizing the new commoditized worker is now the standard, the next decision has to be to decide if you are comfortable being a commodity and what your plan for your commoditization looks like, both now and into the future.

WHORES FOR MONEY?

This is another not-so-nice term I remember hearing about people in general. As an avionics technologist and metrology (metrology is the science of measurement) technologist, I remember my supervisor advising me on career enhancement and on our tendency to work a large amount of "no notice" overtime. When I grumbled about working too much, his answer was that we were all "whores for money".

There have been times when I thought I had gotten away from that analogy, but commoditization has only made the condition worse. In America, it is very true the vast majority of us are motivated by money in almost every decision we make.

As we proceeded through the book, I have tried to consider this situation as we discussed the issues surrounding our commoditization and how many of those issues have to do with money. The connection is quite obvious.

EXPORTING AMERICA'S FUTURE

Since the 1980's, the number of jobs being exported has been steadily increasing. This is a curious condition that has had serious long term impact on a number of American work situations.

While there is no import or export quota for jobs officially, it could be argued that the export of jobs can be compared to the export of any other commodity.

Bearing in mind that the commoditized work force is a large part of the American work force and we continue to export these jobs to other countries, it is possible that we are exporting our future. America is unique in the world in its society, its economy and its work force. When our jobs are exported, either our society goes with it or the product ceases to be an American product.

TRADES WORKERS, MANUFACTURERS AND SERVICE PROVIDERS

Trades workers were a group of people well trained and knowledgeable in their specific trade. They could be found throughout the manufacturing segment in America and formed the backbone of specialties throughout the manufacturing sector.

Manufacturers were companies in place specifically to build things. From sweat shops, to mass production, to custom infrastructure and transportation, these manufacturers were assemblers of goods.

There is now a theory that it is possible to replace these things with a service sector; people who service and repair the items we use. I am not convinced this plan works very well.

UNDEREMPLOYED

How many times do you think about being underemployed?

There was a time when underemployment was not something the average worker needed to think about. So long as the worker remained alive, progression in one's chosen career was an automatic event, only halted when the worker chose to stop, or when a lack of qualifications stopped them. The thought of working below your qualifications was not something to be considered.

With the commoditized workforce, people need to be constantly looking for opportunities. Where in the past the next rung on the ladder might have been a simple matter of tenure, or being the next warm body, now a person must be constantly on the watch for the next engagement and be prepared to market himself into that position. If not, someone else will be marketing themselves.

On the other side, many people still do wait for the next opportunity. With the commoditized market, waiting for the next opportunity to come will mean we become underemployed, or "over-qualified" for the position, but passed over for the boss' job because we did not either appear to want the next level, or were not really looking for the opportunity when it happened.

Underemployment occurs for a number of reasons. Lack of confidence, lack of sleep, lack of time and lack of recognition of talent are a few. A person can trap themselves in a career by languishing in a job that has become comfortable to them. They can become underemployed out of a fear of losing their current position. They can become underemployed through stagnation.

PARENTHOOD IS A CASUALTY?

You will see a reference to this in a few places in my books. I am convinced that parenthood has been a casualty of the commoditized work force. Society's obsession with consumerism and the government's diminishing of a mother's role in successful families has virtually eliminated parenthood as a primary function of those who have chosen to "have" children. Ask any one of them what their primary role in life is and they are not likely to say "parent". Ask any one of them why they work and they will answer "to pay for the house, the car, whatever". Ask any one of them what they wish they had more time for and they are likely to answer something like "more time for my family".

Once again, you can always make more money, but you can NEVER make more time..........

SUMMARY

The workforce in the United States has been commoditized as it transitioned from providing products to providing services. The myriad forces exerting pressure on the labor market have been segmenting labor into sections of commodities and moving the U. S. towards a services economy. Unfortunately, the future for the commoditized worker has been changed. How workers prepare for, engage in and perform their work will be very different from life before they were commoditized.

CONCLUSIONS

Is it possible that consumer goods will no longer be produced in the United States? Is it possible to achieve near full employment based solely on the service economy; repairing all those items made in other countries? A society leaning more toward protecting itself might be a more solid approach, maintaining the strengths of the American economy.

The commoditized job has a different approach. There is less safety and security in the commoditized job market. There are fewer long term opportunities. Producing those items used by Americans with American labor provides the foundation of the American Dream. Without the jobs that come from manufacturing, the trades and all the supporting work to go with them, the commoditized worker will be left alone to prepare themselves to support their families. As they realize their commoditized status, they will need to become their own advocate, a sort of sales department for themselves. In that process, the working class finds itself competing with itself. Commoditization further divides the American population by creating competition between almost everyone in society.

The commoditized job appears to have become the "new normal" for the U. S. working class.

Chapter 14

How To Be A Commodity

Have you made the change yet? Did you even realize you needed to make a change?

We have described what it means to be commoditized and hopefully you have determined whether you have become a commodity. If you have, was it voluntary, or was it thrust upon you?

If you don′t feel you have been commoditized, you have the advantage of preparation.

I believe we have made the case that commoditization is coming to all of us. As the workforce becomes more commoditized, you will need to make changes in your job search methods. You will need to develop ways to keep your resume current. Have you considered how your search for work will need to change?

HOW TO BE A COMMODITY

As you have learned, the commoditization of the American workforce has brought about the need for each individual to be more fully engaged in the management of their job tasks than previously necessary.

It is important that you begin to change the way you look at your career. In almost every respect, the way you market yourself will be a key component. You will no longer wait for answers to applications. Rather, you will actively engage in a full cycle program of constantly updating everything about yourself.

I compare being a commodity to being a generalist. In my career as a healthcare IT consultant, my greatest strength is that I am a healthcare IT generalist. As a commodity, it is more important that a resource fully embrace all aspects of a task. Many tasks previously assigned to another resource simply get missed. Perhaps this is the result of the high turnover of the commoditized worker doing away with the advantage of longevity. Perhaps the commoditized worker simply contributes to the commoditization of all the tasks necessary for employment. Perhaps it is caused by the short assignment duration associated with commodities, which ultimately makes the details unimportant.

Being a commodity is likely to not be something for which you have been trained. In this fairly young segment of the American workforce, there have simply not been rules and designations put in place for this function as compared to the conventional workforce that has been in place for years.

Follow me as we discuss some of the behaviors, styles and attitudes that will allow you to become a better commoditized resource, able to survive in the high churn environment that is the current American workplace. Much of what you read will be obvious. Hopefully, something you read will be a new concept that will make you better prepared to be a human commodity.

DRESS FOR SUCCESS

"You never get a second chance to make a first impression" Many years ago my wife introduced me to a book titled "Dress for Success". In it, John T. Molloy lays out his thoughts on how our method of dress can help us gain success in our lives both personal and business.

This book encourages us to remember our personal appearance at all times. It exposes us to the thought that our personal appearance has impact on our own commitment to our success. It also affirms our knowledge that a personal brand matters.

After reading the book, I slowly changed my mode of dress. I am reminded it is not an inexpensive endeavor. There are ways to make it an easy thing to do over time. It does take a budget commitment to maintain the wardrobe.

I also began dressing in the mirror. To this day, I tie my tie in front of the mirror and stand back for a moment. This reminds me of who I am and the brand I am working to maintain. Sometimes, it reminds me I need a new tie!

As I adopted the dress for success model, I began asking questions. I met a sales person at the clothing store who helped me gain the courage to fully develop a personal reputation for personal dress. I would encourage you to do this sometime. Visit your favorite clothing stores and find a personal consultant to assist you with your personal clothing brand. It may take some work, but it will be worth the effort.

As I became aware of the fact that some could not afford the clothing, I was made aware of thrift stores. While it does take far more time, some effort, and a good tailor, it is possible to upgrade ones wardrobe even when on an extreme budget. As my career goes through its normal highs and lows, it has been very handy to be able to stop in and buy a three hundred fifty dollar jacket for forty dollars......

I have personally seen the upgrade to my career as many of my clients remember me for my mode of dress. During my career, whether I was sitting at a desk, crawling around under a computer, working in a hot room or a cold data center, I at least wore a tie. Even when it was casual Friday (which I personally despise), I elected not to participate. This method had the effect of setting me apart from all the other people in the market. Annoying to some? Probably. Did it ever cost me a job? I doubt it.

When I was in my private consulting practice, much of my referral work came from clients who had become used to me setting a high personal standard. My personal brand first became evident through how I dressed each day. This was the impetus for an upgrade of my demeanor. It also caused me to be more serious about my personal brand.

This was the beginning of a process of establishing a brand that was simply part of the things I did to show the client, other vendors, and peers that I was unique and concerned about providing professional services at every opportunity.

It will be important to be mindful of your appearance at all times. You should keep a cloth around for cleaning your shoes and glasses. Men should shave and maintain a neat appearance always. There will be times when you will unexpectedly encounter someone who can impact your future. I have often met someone at an airport or on a business trip while traveling or sometimes just riding an elevator. I am sure my professional wardrobe helped even when those were casual settings.

Sometimes, the first impression you leave will have to do with how you smell. When it comes to cologne, do not use too much. Too much is any amount that causes a person to look around when you enter their personal space. If you have too much fragrance, you will know. Just watch people for the signs. This is a great place to mention a bad habit. For those of you that smoke, I am sorry, but you need to lose that habit. Nothing is more annoying to a group of non-smoking peers than the smell of cigarette smoke. Just don't smoke when you are in business attire.

CASUAL FRIDAYS

It will be important for you to handle casual Fridays with grace and care as you establish your own brand and go about setting the professional standards you hope your clients come to expect!

In your encounters with others, your ability to communicate your professionalism, manage people and process and enjoy success will first be through non-verbal communication. There is no better way to start that conversation than to dress professionally always. The existence of casual days continues to be argued in business and professional circles. Whatever you do, be sure you have thought it out in advance and that you have decided what your position is going to be when someone comes to you insisting you dress either way.

In my opinion, the childish revolt that is casual Friday causes us to not consider our value to an organization. It also distracts everyone from the task at hand. Arguments for doing it range from the usual "We have done this for years" to "At least I can be comfortable one day a week," to "I don't know why we have to wear a tie, it doesn't make me better at what I do". Well, maybe it does. This is one of the places where a solid, honest self-assessment will help. Watch your own behavior when you "dress down" as compared to when you do not. When you get dressed in the morning, take a moment to look at yourself in the mirror, and try to convince yourself your professional attire has no impact on your professional demeanor. You know it does.

I believe each of these is simply a poor excuse to live to a lower standard. If we are not careful, that standard can result in a lack of respect for the workplace, our fellow employees, consultants, ultimately the client; regardless of whether or not that client is our employer. This is admittedly "old school" as my daughter calls it, but in order to establish ourselves as successful commodities, it is necessary to elevate our thinking about ourselves and our careers. Studies have shown that casual days cause a reduction in production, quality and efficiency on those days:

In an online article entitled "The Effect of Casual Dress on Performance in the Workplace", the point is made: “The way you look directly affects the way you think, feel, and act . . . . When you dress down, you sit down-the couch potato trend. Manners break down, you begin to feel down, and you're not as effective"[72]

Jeffery L. Magee, in his book "America's Going Down The Tube In A T-Shirt", states "Continually relaxed dress leads to relaxed manners, relaxed morals and relaxed productivity" and "leads to a decrease in company loyalty and increase in tardiness."[73]

In my personal experience, I have witnessed a reduction in standards when casual Fridays are implemented. I have also seen quality, quantity and innovation reduced. I have seen a drastic increase in inappropriate behavior and a general reduction in workplace ethics. Of course, some people disagree. I will leave it up to you to decide on which side of the fence you sit.

As part of a personal brand, it is important that you establish yourself as someone who has respect for whatever profession you choose. As a commodity, the first impression may be the only opportunity you have to leave a positive memory. Work to be sure you are setting the proper example and expectations as you go forward in your commoditized career.

POSITIVE ATTITUDE

One of the success concepts that will set a person apart is that of a positive attitude. You will find a number of people who teach this

---

[72] http://www.kon.org/urc/maloney.html

[73] http://www.conselle.com/business-casual-dress-article.php

concept. I am a fan of Tony Robbins and one of his first books, “Awaken The Giant Within”. His enthusiastic and honest approach brings new light into our lives as he exposes us to limitations we impose on ourselves. Many of these things are quite negative and have held us back in our lives and careers. His enthusiasm for introspection and life changing decisions is contagious. Once a person hears him speak of these things, they discover an amazing ability to be free from self-imposed restraints.

Tony Robbins is not alone in his advocacy of positive thinking. There are many successful and helpful resources, any one of which can help us achieve more through positive thinking. I have been involved with Stephen R. Covey, Deepak Chopra and others. Their programs work to provide the tools to keep us self-aware and thinking toward how we might learn, improve and grow. Stephen R. Covey's "Seven Habits of Highly Effective People" is another great book for helping to learn a positive attitude while refining our goal of success.

There is a saying: "You can get farther with honey than you can with vinegar." I have learned that approaching people with a positive attitude produces far better results than approaching them with the opposite. There have been amazing experiences when these attitudes have been adopted and carried out.

I will point out that a positive attitude is not something that can be faked or pretended. When claiming to be a positive thinker, take a look at how you profess that belief. Carefully review your actions and decisions to determine if they reflect your stated belief in a positive outlook.

You are no doubt familiar with this simple test to determine what a person's approach to almost everything will be. Fill a glass to the half-way point with water. Hand it to the person being tested. Without telling them you are testing them, ask them "is the glass half empty, or is the glass half full?" The positive thinking person will say it is half full. You will be surprised how many people do not know about this test.

There are any number of other methods to determine how another person approaches challenges, overcomes adversity or manages difficult projects. It is important to develop a personal positive attitude and to be able to make a rapid determination of the approach of those with whom we work. Seeing the positive components of even the most troubling situation will always produce a better result.

Ask any CEO or executive level person which they would rather be associated with. Most will answer they prefer a person with a positive outlook. In much of what I do, I have found success in hiring personalities with a "can do" attitude. The work is more successful, more fun and more honest.

DO AN HONEST SELF-ASSESSMENT

This is sometimes not an easy thing to do. If you find yourself unfulfilled or feeling like you are not making progress with your career, now would be a great time to do a complete personal assessment or inventory.

That first assessment may take weeks. Keep it available and add to it as additional information comes to mind. Once you have the first version, go over it with someone you trust to give you honest feedback.

This assessment should look at the assets, and deficiencies, you bring to the table. Begin by looking at technical skills, human relations skills, and management skills in the areas you work. Then start the list of things you want to change or make better based on that list. Remember to be honest with yourself. This document will become one of the most important guiding documents for your transformation. It will become a great way to stay focused as you constantly improve your brand.

WHO YOU HANG OUT WITH

This is a terribly elitist sounding subject. It is unfortunate, but who you associate with can tell a lot about who you are. Be careful with those choices. Look at the top 5. Who do you hang out with the most? Do you feel good about that?

One of the first things you should look at would be your personal relationships. Often, these can reveal qualities that might be driving or keeping people away. How do you treat the people in your personal life? How do they treat you? How much do you find yourself emulating those people?

After looking at personal relationships, take a look at work relationships. How do you see other people in the following three categories:

1) Supervisors and managers; those to whom you report and have reporting links to. Do you give them respect, or do you treat them poorly just because they are the boss? When dealing with executives, are you able to see them as people, or do you treat them as royalty?
2) Peers; Those who are in your group of resources with similar functions to yours. Do you take the opportunity to notice the good and bad? Do you apply those lessons in your own approach?
3) Subordinates; In this category "junior" has a sub category, those whose longevity with the company is junior and those whose experience is junior. Are you condescending to them? When you are speaking with them, are you engaged?
Of importance is to always develop a pattern of some level of empathy. This is not to say go soft on subordinates. This does mean taking a hard look at how you treat them and consider how you would feel if you had a boss that treated you that way.
Being a mentor is not something about which many people in supervisory roles think. It is important as you gain experience you give those with less seniority, or even those who are simply struggling, the benefit of your experience and hard learned lessons. If they are willing to receive your counsel and you can deliver it without talking down, your ability to lead is greatly enhanced.

BE AN INNOVATOR

Innovation takes a bit of courage. It takes a willingness to be a pioneer, someone willing to be the first to do something, and not be afraid of the risk that comes with new ideas. Someone who helps to open up a new line of research or technology or art is leading the way for others. As we learn and grow, it is important to find s developmental opportunities, to be creative and to innovate. As we continue to learn and to grow as a commodity, we must be prepared to ask questions. In the process, we will get the opportunity to see things from a different perspective, one that will make us ask "why?" Their "why" is the driving force behind most innovation.

Do you envision yourself as a pioneer? It isn't as hard, or as unlikely, as it may seem. When you have the courage to "call it what it is", you then have an innovative viewpoint enough to also "call it what it is NOT". Once you understand those two things, you can do the analysis that will set your pioneering mind into motion, coming up with a solution.

What do we mean by "Call It What It Is"? Regardless of the task or assignment, whether it is personal or professional, there are times when "what it is" is not what it appears to be. Consider again the story of "The Emperor's New Clothes". Sometimes it will be a very obvious condition. In this story, the town claims to have made the emperor a new set of clothes. Everyone pretends it has occurred. But one person has the courage to "call it what it is" when he proclaims the emperor is walking around in his underwear!

In your professional life, it takes pure courage. If a few people are saying it is one way, but you see it another, what do you normally do? Do you just go along? Is that out of peer pressure? Is it because you don't understand? Or is it because you don't want anyone to think you don't understand?

How many times have you been in a meeting or in a conversation where your boss, your peers, maybe even your spouse, has it all wrong. You sit in the room waiting for someone to correct the mistaken viewpoint but it simply is not happening. It takes courage and conviction to stand up, and maybe stand out, with a group of peers at work, some of whom may intimidate you a bit, but the reward is the ability to drive new ideas and processes. Try it on small things first. You will get better at it.

Transfer that approach to your personal life. With your spouse, it takes enormous courage, along with patience, to decide whether calling it what it is will be worth the effort. Establishing the foundation of truth and honesty in a personal relationship takes finesse and patience. Some people are unable to handle this approach. It will be up to you to decide if it is something your relationship can handle.

Repeatedly in my experience, calling it what it is often brings relief to the conversation and to the relationship. In many cases, people have thanked me after the meeting for saying what they were thinking. Now, my clients know they can count on me to give an honest and professional opinion of the task or process.

Many of the professional successes I have enjoyed have come from this effort (what some might call a quest) to discover the truth in all things. In the case of personal relationships, people have come to expect honesty from me. My spouse has grown used to the idea and I have managed to soften the delivery of some of my thoughts so they do not cause too much trouble.....

Once you have the solution, what is the next step? How do we bring innovation? I propose it is a brave thing to propose new ideas. Combined with knowing who you are and knowing your friends and coworkers, that bravery will allow you to bring successful ideas to implementation with relative ease.

Once we have established the trust that comes from a quest for truth, we are free to seek innovation. Just like being a commodity, innovation takes bravery and courage. It takes someone willing to look at what appears to be "normal" and decide the status quo is not good enough. It takes someone recognizing an idea and believing in that idea until it is fully deployed, or disproved.

Some people call these resources "change agents". There was a time in my career when I despised these people. They would arrive on the scene, do some sort of analysis, issue a few commands, and then leave. Now I am one of those people. It is a great accomplishment to be thought of in these terms. This is the point where, as a commodity, you might go from being a "contractor" to being a "consultant". You are being asked what you think and what your plans are to solve the problem.

FINANCIAL SECURITY

I believe the most important thing we can do to achieve success is to pay off our debts, in particular, to pay off our homes. Paying off our homes early gives us a freedom from the stress that comes from producing a paycheck. The liberating effect of financial security is beyond my ability to describe. You know what I mean when I speak of the concept of being debt free. Nothing brings more security to a person than to know they own their home, to be able to always count on going to that place and not fear being kicked out for not paying the mortgage.

If you have already achieved financial security, try to imagine your life and how it would be different if you had not gotten ahead of the curve early. Keeping empathy in mind, try to see others who still have debt and mentor them into eliminating that debt as their highest priority.

If you are living "paycheck to paycheck" (if you have a mortgage - you are!), then you know the misery that comes with sleepless nights, worrying about the bills and living too close to the financial edge. For those that argue tying your money up in a house is a waste, I would argue they miss the point.

Do all you can do to avoid buying anything on credit. Live so far within your means that people will wonder about your sanity. In these days of instant gratification, it will be tough. But think of the changes that will come with a home that you truly own, not just rent from the mortgage company. Think of the benefit of not having a payment on a car, on a student loan, on credit cards, and what a big difference that would make in your everyday life.

In the book "The Millionaire Next Door", we learn that many multi-millionaires drive very old cars. For instance, Sam Walton, the founder of Wal-Mart drove a 1970’s Ford pickup truck.

Gordon B. Hinckley, the President of the Church of Jesus Christ of Latter Day Saints, has a saying: "Fix it up, wear it out, make it do, or do without."

Think of your life if you had your home and car(s) paid for. There are ways to get there. Develop a plan - and stick to it. Be prepared to live the future you only see in your dreams. Then execute the plan and make it happen. With care and planning, it is possible.

For those just starting on their career path, I cannot possibly overstate the importance of starting out with no debt, and staying that way.

SAVINGS ACCOUNT

As a commodity, it is important that you have a fairly large supply of liquid assets available at a moment's notice. The security that comes from this will be evident as you experience your first phone call telling you the current contract has ended.

I recommend three to six months of income in cash. I keep the cash in a safe deposit box at the bank, in a safe at home, and in my wallet. You might also consider other locations that are safe for storing money out of sight.

With this reserve in place, when you find yourself between gigs, there is no worry and you can focus on getting your next assignment.

If you do not have this savings, you are going to tend to want to take the first job you are offered. You will likely not get the best deal, leaving something on the table in those cases.

WORK/LIFE BALANCE

This is a subject that many people fail to address, yet it is critical to success as a commodity. It is said that when we get closer to the end of our life and ponder on what we might change, it will be rare to hear a person say "I wish I had spent more time at work".

"You can always make more money, but you can never make more time." Remember this phrase. I have deliberately quoted my bishop's phrase multiple times in this book. It is important to achieve the focus that comes from remembering that money is a renewable commodity, time is not.

As a commodity, it will always be possible for you to work more. It will always be possible for you to consider what you might do in order to make your project go better, make that server operate more effectively, get a coworker to adopt your idea, and on and on. That tendency to spend all of your energy on work will ultimately become a distraction as you expend so much energy that it begins to carve away at your psyche. I call this method "brute force". We have all been in this position, we tell ourselves we will just stay an extra 15 minutes today. Then today becomes tomorrow, then your boss wonders why you don't stay that much every day. When that happens, the job owns you. Your actions suggest the workplace means more to you than your own life. "Suicide by Work?"

Sometimes, the very thing you need to be better at your commoditized job will be to leave it behind. There is a popular saying: "When I am at work, I am at work - but when I am NOT at work, I AM NOT AT WORK!" This is a great way to look at yourself as a commodity. It will become a challenge at some point. As your commoditized self is asked to "think outside the box" of a conventional nine to five office desk job, you will see your work creep into your personal time. With laptops, tablets, Androids and Iphones, it is very simple for the work to creep into the "not at work" space.

I normally commit to 45 - 50 hours of work each week. And I try to bill for about 95% of those hours. It has always been a challenge for me to walk away. I have found as I have applied many of the ideas in this chapter, disengaging was a fairly simple thing. Surrounding ourselves with high quality talent, or creating high quality talent is the most effective way to isolate work from personal time. Nothing is so effective at allowing me to go home on time like knowing I have peers and coworkers on whom I can depend .

KNOW WHAT YOU THINK - THINK WHAT YOU KNOW

As my personal life, then my spiritual life and, finally, my career continued to grow, I began to develop my own opinions and thoughts on a wide variety of subjects.

Since my career was in the forefront of a large amount of what I did, I began to "over think" many concepts and ideas. Honestly, I was faking it in a number of conversations where I was adopting the popular thought, often the last one I read, without really thinking of what caused me to take that position. This can be a dangerous approach to one's career. Once it becomes obvious a person will change their position dependent on ambiguous factors, confidence in that person can become damaged.

I remember the first time I had an important interview and gave a very elaborate plan for how to manage the obsolescence of desktop hardware. I took a very aggressive approach, giving the opinion with a detailed description of exact steps and plans. However, when the interviewer dug deeper, I could not dig with him and the plan faltered. It became clear the plan was window dressing without any substance.

It is important to be confident in your thoughts and conversations. It is just as important that you not engage in conversations from which you cannot extract yourself. Another approach would be to simply have a way to extract yourself when you have overstepped reality. One method I use is to simply be truthful : "I am sorry, I have not done enough work in those areas to speak with that level of depth".

It is important to develop a habit of reading new things each day. In most cases, you know what deficiencies you have. Pick up a book and start reading. It will help you overcome any of those deficiencies. Seek out mentors who can fill in the gaps for you. Learning from the mistakes of others is a much more efficient method than learning the lesson personally.

IF IT DOESN'T FIT, FORCE IT

I have worked with a number of people who come up with the

answer first. Then we spent an enormous amount of effort and time trying to make the process fit the result. I refer to this as the brute force mentality. While it can produce results, it is fraught with risk. Some people refer to this as hammering a square peg into a round hole. In most cases, there will be some level of success. The result will often be messy, not organized, and inefficient. There are times when this method should simply not be an option. Call it what it is, then move on.

Often, we do not invest the time or effort to perform a proper and honest assessment of the challenge before executing the solution. Instead we develop and advocate for a solution that has not had a fully vetted experience in theory or practicality. This method is yet another approach where the brute force methodology gets put into place almost accidentally and often without the resources being aware of the dangers. In many cases, the process of working to a defined solution results in churn and burnout, cultivating a systematic contention that is hard to overcome.

Going back to the theory that many business professionals see their careers as a game, they would view their part in the game as either winning or losing rather than as improving or not improving. Many game players get bogged down in this method, taking others down with them in the process.

This is a philosophy you simply have to avoid. If you find yourself in one of these situations, do what you can, learn all you can, and then promise yourself you will not use this method again.

POLITICAL AWARENESS

I know you are wondering why you see this subject in the book, and why so often. Many people do not think politics belongs in a conversation about their short or long term employment. One of my goals has been to encourage all American citizens to (re) engage in the political system.

It is important for us to pay attention to what our government representatives are doing. They are mostly politicians first, then your representatives. They aren't likely to have your best interests in mind because they hear so little from you compared to a list of lobbying resources from corporations, special interests and - yes - the government itself. When you are not engaged, the outcome of this system is often to the detriment of the working class that supports the system.

I encourage you to study the history of the government of the United States. I know such understanding can be somewhat boring at first. For instance, an understanding of the basic structure of the United States government as a Constitutional Republic often reveals characteristics of which many are unaware.

It is incumbent on you to learn the lessons only history can teach. Remember that most of what you think you know is based on a decision someone made in history. Consider the history of labor and corporate America in relation to jobs and careers. There can be no question that the "working class" has never been given priority in decisions about the future of jobs, careers or the "middle class". The very reason this book is necessary is that your government has not had the benefit of your involvement. If it had, the United States would still be the world leader in innovation, quality and productivity; and you would not have been commoditized!

It should be evident it is important to get and stay involved in the political system. It is unfortunate, but many people are "too busy" to even vote. Many people feel there is nothing they can do to change the path we are on. Some will say your involvement is futile, even Quixotic. Get involved; and prove them wrong!

Remember to take the time to go vote every time you get a chance. This is your most important input into our society. The Republic of the United States depends on your activity.

If you want your children and the next couple of generations to struggle as you have, then ignore your obligation as a citizen of The U. S. But be prepared for the backlash as the country implodes after being victim of the citizen's inactivity allowing politicians and special interests to do whatever they want with your future.

There are active, ongoing efforts to make the United States just like every other country in the world. The U. S. was created with a higher purpose in mind. Your political involvement is essential.

DIVERSIFY YOUR SKILLS

In the pre-commoditized world, being a specialist was a viable option. Many of our jobs were extremely specialized. It could be argued that this is one of the things that helped contribute to the demise of production work, maybe even unionized labor.

I mentioned previously my work in the steel industry. These jobs had me banding and otherwise handling coils of steel at a high rate of speed. That was all I did, and it was sometimes extremely monotonous. After a while, I became a hooker, placing the crane hooks in a coil of steel as we lifted the steel out of inventory and loaded it into a slitter. Simple (although that job almost got me killed - but that is a story for another time). In both cases (part of the reason for the downfall of unions), when there was no banding or hooking to do, I sat idle. Yes, I could do more, but the union blocked me from doing some things. If there was no hooker work, I could not help band; I had to wait for the work.

As I look back on those jobs, I realize that there were times when I was not of much value to the organization as a bander. But once I became a hooker, etc, I became more valuable. Why was I more valuable? Because I could function in multiple roles. This also meant that I could easily integrate with someone else in one of those roles because I had done their job.

I tell that story to point out that it is and will always be better for you to diversify your talents. The more things you know, the more things about which you can speak intelligently. Regardless of where you find yourself in your career, the opportunity to learn something new will exist. Whether it is what you "want" to do or not, take the initiative to learn it. This knowledge and experience will be priceless as your career as a commodity matures.

I am a healthcare IT consultant. I tell everyone that will listen that my strength comes from being a healthcare IT generalist first. What I mean by that is I know a little about a lot. The brutal truth is that I am a "Jack of all trades and a master of none." I am perfectly fine with that. In fact, in this world of commoditized labor, this is one of the things that I believe is useful in keeping us employed.

Bear in mind my degree is in avionics. When I got that degree that is all I wanted to do for the rest of my life. Working on airplanes (and flight simulators) was going to be my entire future. So, when choosing a degree path, don't get too hung up on which one. If you ask around, you will find many people who have degrees in a field in which they do not currently work.

STAND FOR SOMETHING

In Gordon B. Hinckley's book "Stand for Something", he exposes us to the true value of standards. While President Hinckley was a religious leader, his recommendations for a good life were absolutely correct.

There can be no question the commoditized job market has contributed to a contentious and difficult work environment, one that often fails to "Stand for Something". To some, this is a risky endeavor. To others, it is simply a nuisance. But if you are going to be a success, an employer will want to know what you stand for. So you need to decide early. You then need to develop a persona that overcomes the contention that comes from leading a team to a standards based destination. So develop a standard, then live up to it at all times.

I have personally seen the destruction done to a person's career when it is discovered they are having an extramarital affair. I have seen the effects on a team that is being ruled instead of being led. I have seen the effects of bad or inappropriate language. Your career will be destroyed if you are seen as a person who believes in the "Do As I Say, Not As I Do" method of leadership. Whether you are formally a leader or not, you ultimately become one. People choose who they follow. Someone will follow you.

If you choose to test this theory, your peers will see the extramarital affair as a weakness. They will either use that knowledge to take advantage, or they will dismiss your guidance as coming from a person who is cheating on their spouse. Aside from the moral reasons, the disregard for human emotion will be felt universally. It will bring up a natural concern for your ability to make decisions, and to treat people as they want to be treated. Using inappropriate language can become a liability as well. My career was impacted by a supervisor who took me aside in an aircraft hangar and informed me my language would keep me from being promoted to a technical lead position. His reason was that my language was inappropriate. Even though I worked in an aircraft hangar with other professionals, many of us chose to use language we brought with us from other sources.

That supervisor handed me a book describing the use of replacement words and informed me I needed to clean up my language or my career was "going nowhere". Regardless of the fact I had enjoyed a tremendous military career, I had a degree in Avionics, was very good at what I did, I ultimately did not receive the promotion because of my bad language.

This is not to say that the standards you pick will be without controversy or consequence. It is quite possible that the standards you choose will either not align with your employer or not be enforceable in an organization. In some cases, your conclusion will be that your standards and those of your employer or supervisor are simply incompatible. In those cases, courage will be necessary as you decide it is time for you to go. I can tell you the relief that comes from resigning a position for which you are not compatible is indescribable, and it points out the importance of always having a solid exit strategy.

In any case, in order for you to find sustainable success, it is your duty to yourself and to the organization to advocate for the standards that you live with every day. Anything less is simply living a lie.

I have often been in situations where action on my part was clearly needed. I believe once you define who you are, you will be satisfied with the results. Don't wait for someone or something to define your standards. Define them early, and then stick to them.

AMERICA FIRST

You cannot go wrong advocating for "America first." After all, you have become a commodity in the American job market. No one knows what the American market looks like in the future. It is a good bet that commoditization is only a step on the way to something else. Remember, commoditization is a natural part of capitalism.

Many have said advocating for preferential treatment for American industry or economy is protectionist. I believe that is true. It is a reality that all governments on the planet are advocates for themselves first. This is as it should be. Why, then, has it become "bad" to advocate for protection of the American free market and the encouragement of domestic production and consumption of domestically produced goods?

I am certain there are forces in the United States economy that are happy the industrialization of America is over. I am sure they look at the U. S. as a source for buying their goods, but not a source for selling them any goods. If you look at who the beneficiaries of the commoditization are, it becomes apparent they are a diversified group that includes the U. S. government, business owners and shareholders. However, it would also include a large component of foreign businesses and governments, some of which have sinister reasons for their relationship with the United States. As we have said, some foreign governments are intent on destroying or, at least, weakening America.

In the future, we will need to be actively engaged in protecting our markets and capabilities just like every other country. But more than that, we need to realize the American economy is unique. Mixing the economies of socialist, aristocratic, dictatorial regimes with ours puts our way of life in jeopardy.

Be patriotic regardless of the backlash. It is your right and obligation to show loyalty to your country. This is, after all, the country that makes your life, and that of your family, possible.

CALL IT WHAT IT IS

Many organizations struggle with the discovery of the truth. I am sure you have worked for someone whose claims did not line up with truthful assessments of their results or actions.

It is important to develop a way to recognize the truth, and then communicate that truth. As I stated earlier, my mantra has become "Call It What It Is, Then Kill Them With Kindness". This has worked well for me as I have been blessed to be asked for my opinion on a number of solutions. It did not always work well. Once I developed this approach, I had to refine a communications method that worked as well. Delivering the awkward news that something is not as it appears takes finesse combined with courage.

There is freedom in adopting this approach. There is no more trying to figure out what your position is for which audience. There is no more remembering what you said about a particular matter. There is no more struggle with finding the "real" cause for a problem, regardless of whether it is for business or personal reasons.

Root Cause Analysis is a great tool for this method. Simply create a few lists to keep around and where those lists differ work to discover the truth. Then once you have all the facts , even different facts from different parties, you can feel comfortable in speaking the truth.

DEVELOP A PERSONAL BRAND

When someone asks you what you do, what do you say? When they ask how you do it, what do you say then?

Do you really know the answer to these questions? Take the time to develop your personal brand. How you dress, how you speak, how you treat other people, what expectations you set are the things that people talk about after you leave the room.

When your name comes up in a meeting (and it will), what do you want people to think of first? Your personal brand includes most of the things we have covered in this chapter. From your dress, to your honesty, to your ability to be loyal to the standards you set, people will recognize your brand. If that brand is not what you intend, develop a plan, and fix it quickly!

You will develop a reputation that will become the core of your brand. For instance, if you have a reputation for a policy of "Do what I say, not what I do", your brand will bring you nothing but failure. But if you develop a brand of being trustworthy and of providing successful solutions, there will be more opportunities than you will be able to handle.

Try this exercise. For an entire day, when someone mentions a person's name, write it down. Then, write a word or sentence that reflects the first thing you think of when you hear that name. Be honest. At the end of the day, review the list. If you have been honest, some of those things will be nice, and some will not be so nice.

Then think, if my peers, coworkers, family members, even

strangers were asked to perform this exercise about me, what would they say? Again, if you are honest, you already know the answer. Will this be the image you intend to leave in the minds of others?

As a commoditized resource, a consultant, your entire professional existence depends on what people think of you. When a meeting occurs and your name comes up, what do you want people to say about you? Is that who you are?

If it is not who you really are, you have some work to do. Or you need to change the brand. Nothing will destroy your career more rapidly than having a reputation as a dishonest or untrustworthy resource, or even a reputation as someone you are not.

Cultivating a personal brand can take time. Once it is in place, it is hard to remove or change. Take your time. Don't be afraid.

Develop the brand, and then make the changes necessary to be true to yourself and to the brand. Then, have the courage to be what you claim to be.

Finally, this is one place where you should NOT actively promote the brand. Self-promotion is OK for a singer or an actor, or a book writer. It is NOT OK for a consultant. If you develop and cultivate your brand correctly, you will see the promotion occurring, but it will not be you doing the promoting; it will be everyone with whom you come in contact.

BE PREPARED TO MAKE HARD CHOICES

A very good reminder of how to approach the management of our careers is that sometimes we just have to make hard choices. I recently left a very good position as a manager where I had been blessed to overcome politics, infighting and the other standard "negatives". I was chosen as part of a new “director's team”, garnering great support and success as I worked into a solid position that was the envy of many of my peers.

I remember the days and weeks where I realized the 15 hours a week in the car were competing with my family time at home and with my efforts to write my biography. I remember the absolute angst of deciding to leave a full time position to go back to consulting. I remember the sheets of paper with pros and cons on them and how, no matter how hard I tried to make the career come first, family always won out.

I recall having to tell my good friends and peers - even my boss - that it was time for me to go. I recall sleepless nights worrying about my friends and team members and how I would appear to have let them down.

For awhile, I had the opportunity to contribute remotely as a consultant while fixing my children breakfast, picking them up from school, attending butterfly launches and Christmas parties at the elementary school, picking up a sick child, going to lunch with my wife and children. I never wonder if I made the best decision! As I receive many wonderful recommendations on Linked In from past friends, I miss the old "job" tremendously. So, I occasionally look at my list of pros and cons as a reminder of why I made the change. Sure, I miss the friends, coworkers and even the "prestige" of being a manager at the second largest health care company in the United States. Then around 2:30, I get in my car, sit in line with all the other parents, pick my kids up and take them for an ice cream cone on the way back to my "office" at home.

This approach can work for business decisions as well. There will be times when the decision has an impact on you or on someone with whom you have a great rapport. The scoring method below will reveal what needs to be done after you have done an honest evaluation.

I suggest when the change looks possible or necessary, we go back to basics. A simple piece of paper with two columns, one labeled "pros" and one labeled "cons". Stick that piece of paper in your pocket and when a "pro" or "con" regarding your career decision comes up, pull it out and write that down. After about two weeks, sit down and type that into a spreadsheet. Assign a score to each item based on the priorities you have set for your work/life balance. Then sum the columns. There is your answer. Then, develop a plan and don't look back! It will be the right thing to do.

COMMON COURTESY

A little common courtesy will go a long way in your branding effort. Open doors for people. Take the next elevator. Bring someone some candy. Take the time to write a personal note. In the end, these things will open doors for success at every level.

Say "Please" and "Thank You". I will admit I learned this philosophy as an Air Force brat. For years, I fought against it.

Never when my parents were around, because you never argue with your career Air Force father!

This philosophy has worked out well. It will serve you well as you go about accomplishing things through the use of common courtesy.

It will not always be an easy thing to do. To say thank you to someone who has just raked you over the coals for a two hour meeting will be difficult. The sooner you are able to do that, and mean it, the sooner you disarm your antagonist and get down to the business of managing whatever you are doing.

BE A CONSULTANT, NOT A CONTRACTOR

In these days of commoditization, opportunities come in different forms.

With the commoditization comes recruiting firms. Recruiters work hard to provide their clients, ultimately your clients, the best commodity – (again, that's you) - to fill their need.

As a commodity, you will be tempted to start referring to yourself as a contractor. Many of your clients will use that term to describe your role. It is possible you might start referring to yourself that way as well.

If you are doing this correctly, you will discover you are more than a contractor. In most cases, you are a specialist. Your skills are needed to come in and take command of a situation, applying your in depth knowledge and experience to bring the issue to a successful conclusion.

When I was working in aviation, I learned a saying that applies well to consulting: "You are not paying me to turn screws; you are paying me to know which screw to turn."

As you develop as a commodity, it will always be important to behave as a consultant to the organization. This assumes a more professional demeanor and outlook. It is a more positive part of your brand that tells the client, and those around you, you are serious about providing a solution. The client gets a constant reminder that he has hired a professional to come in and solve his problem.

As a consultant, you represent a profession. A consultant provides an honest and truthful assessment of the client's operation, provides or recommends solutions, and executes a game plan. I often refer to myself as a "hired gun" or as a healthcare IT consultant. This upgrade always elicits a smile from the client and brings a look of confidence to the client's face.

Why do it? Why be a commodity that prefers to be referred to as a consultant? Isn't it risky? Isn't it scary? You bet. But the rewards are great. In the commoditized world, it is the new reality.

How great is it to have more latitude and to be able to enjoy a fuller life by providing for yourself and your family? If handled correctly, a consultant has a more secure future. Certainly one can expect more time with one's family. What freedom comes from financial security?

There is also a sense of accomplishment not available to many in this commoditized society. To be handed a large project and entrusted with success is large enough. But then to be able to leave that successful project and go on to the next challenge is one of the ultimate successes! Behind the successful raising of children, what more satisfaction can there be?

CERTIFICATIONS

Certifications can serve to help your career and your branding particularly if you are less experienced. Much like a diploma or a degree, they can do two things for you. First, they show you are committed to your own education. Second, they show your general aptitude for a specific subject or career field.

Certification in a specific area can give a person the validity they need with an employer. In obtaining the certification or additional knowledge, a person often gains some experience. We also generally gain networking experiences and, in the perfect situation, we will gain access to the people who can help us find the "side door" to that new opportunity.

I personally have allowed many of my certifications to lapse or expire. I have also hired many professionals who no longer have certifications. But they have the one thing that trumps certifications and a degree – experience. If a person has been in a particular career field for a lengthy time and can provide multiple examples of success, that person has advanced to the period in their career where the certifications and degree do not mean as much.

Before you dismiss this opinion, allow me to mention that many of the people who now have experience got it specifically because they had the credentials at one time, or took the initiative to learn the material during their career, which is a much slower way to obtain that career.

SUMMARY

The commoditized job market requires a new way of thinking and acting towards every aspect of a person's career. From filling out the application, to maintaining a resume, to the networking so critical to success, the job of maintaining a job has changed. With the changes in what we do to support ourselves comes a requirement to be constantly reinventing ourselves. It is important that we be willing to learn, to do the best we can and to constantly determine the value we bring to our commoditized product. As a commodity, we are always in competition for the next opportunity.

CONCLUSIONS

Being a commodity requires a different approach to your short and long term career goals. It also requires activity in areas previously viewed as off limits. As a commodity, it will continue to be important to recognize what makes you valuable – and refine those characteristics as necessary.

Chapter 15

How To Find Your Next Job

Finding your next job may take an extended effort in the commoditized job market. Consider what you need to do in order to be successful at remaining employed.

ENGINEER YOUR RESUME

You should understand a few things about your resume. In the commoditized labor market, you should give your resume a solid review and assessment. Once it is complete, constant refinement will be critical:

1) This could be the most important document in your portfolio. But it might not be if it is not properly reviewed and integrated with your entire personal brand. In concert with your registration on a few on-line websites, it can be invaluable. If, for instance, your Linked In resume differs from your paper resume, you will have some explaining to do if you get a call.

Getting a properly engineered resume requires us to read the resume as if we were the hiring authority. Don't view it as a technical document, view it as an article, or even as an advertisement. Your resume has to reach out and grab the reviewer or hirer in order for it to serve the purpose of getting the reader's attention.

2) Remember that if all you have done is send resumes to hiring companies, your chances of getting the job interview are severely reduced. As effective as this method once was, it no longer holds value. I know it will be tempting to blast your resume out to anyone for whom you have an address. While you are at it, go buy a couple dozen lottery tickets; similar odds apply.

3) If you think your resume is going to stand out because you printed it on colored paper or used a different font, think again. Remember, technology makes the first pass at most resumes. So anything that depends on human intelligence to discriminate is lost before you get started. In some cases, color and unique fonts actually make the document more difficult to read using artificial intelligence.

4) Once your resume gets in the stack, what makes the hiring authority pick you? These people view hundreds of resumes. What makes yours stand out? Remember, there are a large number of resources going after fewer and fewer jobs. Why would YOU hire you? Your resume must include a truthful and factual single sentence introduction followed by a short two paragraph summary right up front. It needs to tell the reader what your personal brand is, and sell it, quickly! Leave off the gimmicks and buzz words. People don't necessarily hire based on that stuff.

5) If you are not fully qualified for or matched to the job for which you are applying, you are wasting effort.

Technology now checks most documentation before a human gets to it. So it is vital to your efforts that you figure out how to effectively use the proper descriptive words to start up the process. Be sure you know what you say you know. If this method gets you past the first pass, the second pass is going to want evidence. An interviewer will go to technology like Linked In and double check your story. Good interviewers will be able to see through a lie very quickly. Whatever you do, do not tell a lie on your resume.

6) If you spent less than an hour putting together a simple chronological list of your jobs, that is not going to be an effective resume. A resume for an entry level person should take at least 2 hours to assemble. Combined with on-line efforts on Linked In and other places, a person new to the commoditized market could easily spend tens, maybe hundreds of hours on the resume effort. Once you are a seasoned commodity, it will still take one or two hours each week just to maintain your online presence and keep your resume fresh, after you have spent up to 100 hours getting it right to start with! Remember, the worst time to refresh your resume is after you have been released from your previous assignment. As your opportunities and responsibilities change, get it into the resume. I personally review my resume every week to ensure my successes are adequately reflected in the document. Likewise with Linked In, I spend at least 10 minutes every morning going through my profile, answering emails, and commenting on interesting articles.

7) Don't obsess over page count. Initially, I worked very hard to keep my resume down to a single page. I have seen others try to do

that as well. Leave that idea as a secondary issue. Provide an honest overview of your abilities first, and then see where it fits. My current resume is five pages long, and hiring folks do read it all! If the first page looks solid and builds a case for your services, the hiring authority will want to read whatever you put in the document. Just don't waste their time.

Build An Impressive Resume

Building an impressive resume takes a large amount of time, extreme attention to detail and lots of care. It also takes a very specialized talent and an intimate knowledge of the area in which you are being commoditized. Be prepared to make this a part of your life. The more you dedicate yourself to the effort, the more likely you will achieve success.

My religious affiliation (The Church of Jesus Christ of Latter-day Saints) puts on career seminars geared towards under and unemployed members of the community. What began there as a review of my resume turned into an obsession very quickly as I worked to refine and improve the document. After the first six months or so, I became a bit frustrated with the process. While mine was a good resume, something was simply missing. I was receiving some interest, but I felt the document did not adequately represent me. It certainly was not giving me a competitive advantage.

Even though my family and I could not afford the cost, we hired a company to tweak my resume. They performed an initial no cost evaluation of the resume and sent me notes on a number of things I needed to improve in the content of the resume. They assured me they could help and very carefully introduced me to concepts and processes that made my resume better. I was concerned they were giving me the standard sales pitch. When I mentioned it, they were very straight forward. I would get better responses, or they would refund the price. Our financial circumstance was so poor we had to save up and make payments on the service, but the investment paid off. In both the short and long term, their advice made an enormous impact on my efforts.

The results of the resume company's efforts were simply stunning. The flow of the document was much smoother. The structure of the document was completely different. It clearly had a more professional look and feel. It also bragged about me in a way I could never have done myself. It also represented me very well in a rapid fire format.

It was just a couple of weeks after I received the "new" resume I began getting calls from companies and individuals that I had been frustrated with gaining access to before. That simple resume continues to be the foundation of my resume to this day. It was a solid investment for me and worth every dime. I made that investment back in a matter of just a few months.

What I learned was that while my old resume was technically accurate and indicated my broad background very well, there was no excitement in the delivery. It didn't jump off the page at the reader. It spent all of the reader's time simply delineating (boring) technical detail. What needed to happen is that the resume needed to set me apart from everyone else. It needed to do that within just a few seconds of the reader picking it up.

I learned that I have about 30 seconds to present something that caused my resume to move from the "pass" to the "keep" pile. So, in addition to the buzz words and usual demographics, I had to include qualified and quantified facts about my work, including specific successes. Hesitant to be seen as a braggart, I had never been comfortable with self-promotion about my work, but it was what was needed.

I recommend that you engage all the resources at your disposal to review and perfect your resume. At some point, you may be blessed to be able to afford to hire someone to take a look at your resume. There are plenty of folks to do this; many will do the analysis at no cost. Attend every class you can find on employment tactics and leave all your preconceived notions behind. Study successful people as well. Many of them will be happy to offer you advice and otherwise mentor you on the process.

Then be prepared to become your own special advocate. As a commodity, you are now responsible for the marketing of your services as much as any commercial business. Your ability to sell yourself through all the means you have at your disposal is vital in securing your future.

AN HONEST SKILLS AND APTITUDE ASSESSMENT

The first thing that you absolutely need is to know yourself well.

This is no small task. Most people have trouble doing an honest self assessment. It takes time to slow down and do the assessment. It also is helpful to have a trusted friend or two who can help you see all of your strengths and weaknesses.

The next thing you should do is to try to find an aptitude assessment test. I personally feel these should be regularly administered to children from about sixth grade in order to determine their natural inclinations. The results of these tests are often very enlightening and definitely helpful in determining the weak areas on which you will need to work. These assessments will also reveal what your natural talents are. Nothing is less productive than pounding a square peg into a round hole. Had I not become aware of my technical talents (left brain) I might have spent my life forcing myself to do something for which I had no natural ability.

Create and maintain a skills inventory with a score. You may do this with a simple spreadsheet. You need three columns - skill, score, and left/right/both. The score should reflect any preferred skills you may feel make you a better candidate for your "dream job." Do not be afraid to list everything you know, no matter how minor. You may tweak it later. Mine had a column I could check for applicability to the job for which I was applying. The left/right/both column is to help sort out which brain skills are required to go with the stated skill.

Scoring that sheet can be a little subjective and will take time. It will allow you to establish relationships between all of your talents and what they say about your skills inventory. This is a three dimensional effort with all of the items having an impact on all of the other items. Be prepared to spend some time here as well.

LEFT BRAIN VS RIGHT BRAIN

I was personally the beneficiary of the results of an ASVAB test I took fairly late in my career. As a 25 year old father of three working as a used car mechanic, I met a man who was a supervisor at an Air National Guard base in Nashville, Tennessee. In the process of working on his car, Tom Gober engaged me in a conversation about what I intended to do with my future.

Tom convinced me to go to the recruiting office and discuss enlistment in the National Guard. I distinctly remember taking the ASVAB. The almost immediate call that came from the recruiter informing me I had an aptitude for electronics. That was a key for me to gain access to one of the most sought after training programs in the military. Tom Gober would be a mentor and leader to me for a number of years as I excelled in the field of avionics and ultimately achieved the rank of Tech Sergeant E6. His leadership also led to my obtaining a degree in avionics.

Throughout junior high and high school, I had been fully engaged in the musical studies. I limped along through school and barely graduated from high school. Not because I was not smart, but because I was simply bored. I continued working towards a degree in music after high school, but really was not good enough to pursue that career as I encountered true musical talent in my chosen studies.

Functionally, I had always been blessed by a father who had passed down his "Jack of all trades, master of none" talents to me. Many of the jobs I had held were left brained, but I really had no thought of the difference between left brain and right brain. This has been learned the hard way - and certainly is a result of the perfect vision that only hindsight can offer.

Music is clearly a right brained activity and I had no idea I had left brained talents and aptitude. As I have learned, many engineers have some level of musical talent. My ability to play music was purely because music is, at its core, a numbers game. As I look at it now, it is quite clear; I could play, but I could not sight read the music. I could play almost anything and any type of music, but I could not write a note. Even today, I can sing, but I cannot sing from the music.

I mention this because it is important to know what your natural skills are as you look at your skills inventory. An honest assessment will take into account your natural abilities in deciding where your strengths lie.

It will be important that you know this about yourself as you embark on this journey. It is true your next client or employer will need to know, and be able to tell. It will be more important that YOU know, so you may work to fully leverage your talent in the proper way.

In my career, I am often asked "Are you a doctor"? My response is to smile and say "Why yes - yes I am! I am a doctor of computers"! While being a physician takes a specific natural skill set, so does being a Healthcare IT Consultant. In order to know and appreciate the impact our natural abilities have, we must have completed an assessment of what our natural talents are.

PRACTICE, PRACTICE, PRACTICE

It is a good idea to practice interviewing for a job. It is also a good idea to gain practice as the interviewer. It has been an immense help to me. I very deliberately continue my job search on a ongoing basis. This helps for a number of reasons:

INTERVIEWING WITH EMPLOYERS

We all need practice. This is one of the best ways to know what works and does not work for us personally. In this effort, there is no such thing as failure. I always take a fairly new looking notebook with me (I never take technology into an interview). That notebook might be for notes about the job, but the truth is I make notes about what I did or did not like about the interview. I also note what I did and did not do in the interview. It is also an easy way to take control of the interview. It keeps the interviewer off balance a little as you jot down notes at opportune moments. These notes have proven quite valuable in the process of interviewing. Even when I am employed, I occasionally take an interview just for practice. They also can make great networking opportunities!

INTERVIEW WITH EMPLOYEES

When I say we all need practice, I mean all of us. The interviewer is often not happy about the process. By interviewing with these people, the interviewer gets practice and insight on their methods as well. Whether they realize it or not, they gain needed practice when I go on a "dead end" interview.

I have met people with whom I interviewed some time later in my career. We often talk about the interview, how I was not a fit and how it helped them to have the opportunity to interview me.

I also have made some great contacts and friends in these meetings. There is nothing wrong with realizing early that you have converted an interview to a networking opportunity. The manager will be impressed, I promise.

This will take hard work and dedication. You need to develop a pattern of going on interviews as much as you can. The experience will help you assess diverse experiences and interview styles. In addition, it will give you confidence as you go through more interviews, you will learn how to "read the room". You will begin to recognize the styles you are encountering. You will become adept at recognizing when the opportunity is not right for you. This will free you to be your real self. You will get the opportunity to then change the tide in an interview by relaxing with the interviewer. Imagine their surprise when you release the energy and emotion from the interview by changing the subject to family, or sports, or even politics! It is a great feeling to take command of an interview and determine your own destiny by releasing the interviewer and leaving the interview clearly in charge of the discussion. This will elevate your self esteem, and often will leave an indelible mark in the mind of the interviewer. Most of the time, if you go out of your way to leave an image of yourself with someone, it will be a positive mark.

You need to experience different interview styles. Regardless of how much you read or study about them, nothing is better than living through a few of them.

Practice gives you an opportunity to "see behind the curtain". It is often quite difficult to remember that the interviewer is a real person. Many interviews are heavily impacted by those psychological efforts in which many managers engage. The more you watch, the more likely the curtain will part and you will see it is only a human back there.

I once worked quite hard just to get a group interview at the nation's largest health care company. I had very little hope of actually getting the job. I simply wanted to have the chance to participate in a group interview like this company was known to perform.

It was actually a very frightening experience. But I learned something. I learned that I don't do group interviews. I also learned that group interviews are quite intimidating, by design. I learned that in the case of the company I interviewed with, the interviewers had practiced a method of interviewing that was quite deliberately intense, deceptive and stressful. I also learned I had better learn more about the process. I studied, asked friends about them, and decided I personally was not a fan of group interviewing. As a result, I no longer have aspirations of working for that company.

I have enjoyed great success using this method to set up practice interviews in a number of places. The practice has always been good for my interviewing, my interview style, and for my career in general.

Even when I am engaged in a contract, I continue to interview at least once each month. If a recruiter emails, calls, or sends me a note on Linked In or other social media, I make it a point to call or email them and thank them for the opportunity.

DON'T CRY

During your interview, it is very important that you not turn your story into a pity case:

1) Don't tell stories about being picked on, or about the latest conspiracy to hold you back.

2) Don't beg for the position, make a case for your selection

3) Don't talk about how much you need the job....... ever!

Positive attitude is everything in these situations. Your job is to convince the interviewer you are exactly what they need. This requires knowledge, salesmanship and confidence.

In order to do this, you need to make it all about the employer. Don't focus on your problems. Even when asked, have answers ready; answers you have already worked out in advance.

CONTROL THE CONVERSATION

I don't mean you should be rude. I mean you should have a commanding presence. The interviewer wants to know you can control almost any situation, regardless of what you are engaged in doing for the business. A commanding presence gives the employer confidence you can perform your tasks, and that you are confident you can perform them! But that commanding presence also gives the employer something to think about as they consider how your futures intertwine.

This skill, particularly for left-brainers, can be something that will take a large amount of time, effort, training and practice. Conversation, even about technical subjects, is a right brain activity. The skills you need to be able to make a conversation flow well will need to be practiced. They will also require a commanding knowledge of basic subjects and a broad knowledge of nearly everything, including current events.

This knowledge is something you will have to work to acquire.

GET TO KNOW PEOPLE

It is not easy to read some people. It is a skill that takes work to really be effective. There was a time when I was not a "people person". With practice and exposure, I have been able to get better at it.

It will be an asset for you to become a student of human behavior. Regardless of your role in life, you will be able to have more control, be more effective and leave a better impression once you are able to fully understand what all the players expect from you. This takes a deep understanding of the behavior and motivation of individual people.

For instance, some will want truth. Some will want fluff. You have

15 seconds and maybe one question to figure which type they are. The sooner you figure it out the better.

Here is another place where your personal brand will have extreme value. Often, a person's ability to communicate their personal brand will determine how much they can gather about another person, and how much of it is the truth.

FIND THE SIDE DOOR

Let's suppose you apply for a job that you feel is a perfect fit for you. But you are not certain you fit the exact requirement. The computer making the decision about who to hire may pass you by based on any number of criteria. Your resume or application will go into the very large stack of paper to which the less than perfect candidate's profile is relegated.

This is when you will need a side entrance. Here again will be the importance of personal brand and a large amount of networking. You will also benefit from keeping all of your personal contacts up to date. The candy and lunch budget will pay off as you are able to walk into the side door on a position and get an audience with someone directly.

BE A MENTOR

There are a number of reasons for being a mentor. I have personally been the beneficiary of mentoring on a number of occasions. The first few times, I had no idea that was what the person was doing. Over time, I have discovered this wonderful concept. As I look back over my career, I see the influence of those mentors in many places.

Mentoring takes deliberate effort in order to help people achieve all they can. In the world of commoditized labor, this mentoring will be critical as we each become responsible for our own talents and knowledge.

MAKE THEM WANT YOU

Study the work force and decide what value you bring to the relationship. Don't walk into an interview without a full and complete understanding of what the employer is looking for. Once you have that understanding, make them want you.

DON'T TALK ABOUT MONEY

During the interview process, stay away from discussions of money. Once you have made them want you, be prepared to play it cool. This takes planning, and bravery!

Once you establish with an employer or contract agency what your price is, they have the upper hand. So don't talk about it. Make them come to you. Many contract agencies will ask you up front "What is your rate?" It is very important that this conversation be as short as possible. If you say $20 per hour and they say $12, you need to have already decided what your response will be. If it is no, then say no, and get off the phone interview. If it is yes, do likewise. If it is maybe, you have 30 seconds to change it to a yes or no. If you cannot, have an exit speech ready, and make it good.

YOU HAVE 15 SECONDS

When encountering people in your networking efforts, remember you have 15 seconds to make that first impression that may never be retracted. "You never get a second chance to make a first impression".

KNOW WHAT YOU ARE WORTH

You may think you know what you are worth. That is simply not enough. This is a good time to remember you have become a commodity.

I once had a car that I thought was worth twenty seven hundred dollars. It had a new engine and tires and it was a pretty nice ride. For weeks, we listed the car in many venues. We put it on Craigslist, we told our friends, we emailed people and I posted it on my website. Still nothing. We lowered the price one hundred dollars, then another hundred. What a frustrating process. We still got no calls.

Finally, we did more research. We looked it up on a couple of different websites and we ran some comparisons on other vehicles. We put a more reasonable price on the car based on our research. Within a week, the car was sold.

Think of yourself as that car. Being a commodity is the same thing. Your economic value to the employer is determined by the same qualities as the car. But before you can have that conversation, you have to be realistic about your market value.

Once you have established a reasonable and realistic view of what you are worth, you need to find market value. How do you do that? This is another activity that will take an extensive amount of work on your part.

You should begin by creating a list of your talents and skills. Remember, you are a commodity, so this list needs to include the tasks for which an employer is willing to pay.

At some point you will want to go to salary.com and research what your talents are worth. This also will require a bit of effort as you take the time to present honest data as correctly as possible.

Finally, find people who do what you want to do and ask them.

In the end, you will have a detailed, realistic list of your value to any enterprise. If it is not enough money, it is time to study what you may do in order to increase your compensation. In the meantime, it will be time to start shopping for the job that will get you by. This will be your time to build the core of your personal brand and skill set.

When deciding on a career path, don't limit yourself too much. I know, you have decided you want to be a manager; but don't be afraid to take work as a technician. The skills you learn will always make you a better manager.

When I first found myself being serious about finding a job and nurturing my market brand, I sought out the advice of others. One of the people I spoke with was a very successful director of an aviation company. We were speaking about salaries when he told me the key to success. As we talked about the subject, he said "Get it going in, because if you don't you may never see it."

This was the beginning of a unique approach for me. Separate the discussion of the job and its tasks from the discussion about compensation. Then whatever the salary needs to be, "Get it going in."

Remember when an employer tells you they want you, but their budget is tight, they are asking YOU to help fund THEIR operations! If it appears they need your help and you can actually help them, you may consider a contribution by working for less compensation initially, but you should be compensated with a better bonus. Remember – get it going in, or you will never see it! I will say of all the opportunities I have had to take less than I wanted, or to take some sort of deferred compensation, not one of those events turned into a good experience.

EXUDE CONFIDENCE

Be confident in what you do. Don't lie to yourself, or to anyone else. Take a hard and honest look at what you are capable of, and then be as good at it as you possibly can be. Watch other people who are employed doing what you want to do. Learn from their successes, and their mistakes.

Then, know you can do that thing and be confident when speaking of it.

Then, simply add to the list of things of which you are confident.

READ A LOT

Read as much as you can. Get to know as much as you can about as much as you can. Not to show off or bring attention to yourself, but the more conversant you are at a large variety of issues, the more likely it is you will be able to have a conversation about a subject with a person who may have the power, authority or connections to find you your next job.

Reading is, for me, an opportunity to focus. This, too, takes work. I also need to read from a physical book. I have every electronic device known to man, but there is nothing so pleasant as having a book in my hand from which to read.

EXPAND YOUR VOCABULARY

Improving one's vocabulary is a fairly simple thing to do. My parents had me read a page a day from the dictionary when I was a little boy. That helped me tremendously with spelling and with diction. It also helped me with a broad vocabulary. I have a personal habit even now, looking up a word if I am even the slightest bit unsure of its meaning. With such open access to the Internet, it is much easier today to look up a word heard, but not understood completely.

SELECT GOOD FRIENDS

I have made many great friends across the spectrum of industries. As a Rotarian, I met many people who would later open doors for me in a variety of settings.

As an entrepreneur, I met many people as well. I know attorneys, doctors, educators, financiers and others - most of whom will have lunch with me with a single phone call.

Most of these people are good friends of mine and we always have enjoyable conversation. Rarely do I need to ask them for a favor because I keep them up on what I am doing. They also keep me up on their projects and there have been times when I have been able to help them.

These friendships are invaluable.

You may have read in one of my other books, "From The Strip Club To The Temple" about my early experience with a term "You all think you are better than we are." Similar to elitism and dangerously close to being judgmental, it is simply something I have had to get used to. The fact is that there are some people with whom being friends is not a positive experience, and can be a hindrance! Identify these people early, and let them go !

DO YOUR RESEARCH

It is important that you know the position you have applied for as well as the company you are applying to. This will take intense research using all of the skills we have discussed, from networking, to brand management, to attendance at conferences, you will need to take a proactive part in researching all you can about the positions in which you are interested.

Who is hiring? What positions are being filled? Are the positions fulltime, part-time, contract or contract to hire? Who do you know working there?

DEVELOP YOUR PERSONAL BRAND

We have already determined a personal brand is important to your total career plan. The days of identifying your skills and waiting for someone to offer you a job have been replaced with a need to set yourself apart from the competition. The best way to do this is with a solid approach to what you are offering each opportunity.

This will take a different approach. The first thing to remember is that "everything is sales". Your brand is your first marketing piece. Make sure that brand is customized to the needs of each open position.

When someone hears your name, what is the first thing they think of? How will you know? If the answer is not what you need/want it to be, how can you change it for the better? How can you manage that fifteen second rule related to your brand?

This is where networking will be important once again.

Associating with as many people as you are able will give you a broader choice of career options. It will also give you a broader group from which to get your brand definition.

Searching for the next commoditized job will include a large amount of preparation as those jobs become scarcer and require more diversified skills. Focusing on the future and reaching out to all of your contacts on a regular basis could be the difference between employment and becoming a statistic in the labor force participation rate.

BE AN ENTREPRENEUR

What the United States needs is leaders, not managers. What made the United States great was a combination of a minimally invasive Constitutional government and citizens who were unrestrained in their ideas. I know it is a scary time, and the thought of risking everything to be an entrepreneur is not for everyone, but you must include this in your choices.

Do you have ideas about the proverbial better mousetrap? Do you feel you have advanced knowledge or experience in a trade? I propose as a commoditized worker there can be no better time to be an entrepreneur.

It is true with government regulation and taxation at historically high rates, and with very little personal lobbying for your effort, there can be some sleepless nights. But the rewards both personally and financially could be enormous as you embark on the trip to make the world better through entrepreneurship.

SUMMARY

The development of a strategy to find your new job will take an enormous amount of effort – and it is hard work! As we become a more commoditized society and changes come into our work force, it will be extra important to be fully engaged so you recognize and adjust for the changes in the market. Because of this, it will be important that you can do what you say you can, and that what you can do is in high demand.

Many times, people do not hire skill, they hire personality. As the job market shrinks and the middle class disappears, obtaining a job will become a larger challenge. What sets you apart? Are your talents going to last for thirty or forty years?

CONCLUSIONS

Commoditization has changed every aspect of a career in the United States.

Finding a career and a job requires diligence in networking, brand management, skills maintenance and salary negotiations. Starting with the resume, we must remember that we are each battling for fewer and fewer jobs that will allow us to support and prepare our families for the future. As a commodity, our value is in danger of being minimized. It is important to know the market and be prepared to change as commoditization changes everything we do to survive in the commoditized world.

Chapter 16

What About The Future?

Having learned of the commoditization syndrome, I am sure you now have many questions about what the future looks like for those who remain in the workforce in the United States. This chapter will attempt to give you a view into the future of the American workforce. It will also give you a look into the possible scenarios that could occur and what elements of society could cause those events.

RIGHT TO WORK?

Have you heard the term "Right To Work"? In your busy life, have you bothered to stop and ask what that term means? The establishment and the government would have you believe this would give you some right you previously did not have. Nothing can be farther from the truth.

In the United States, everyone has the right to work. In parts of the United States, organized labor helped create laws to restrict where the work came from, but everyone had the right to work. In actuality, what it means is you no longer have the right to collectively bargain for wages, benefits and working conditions, even if you need the ability to negotiate fairness on those issues.

So, while corporate America and your government work to convince you "Right To Work" is in your benefit as a laborer, nothing could be farther from the actuality. Whether you agree with the point of unions or not, you have just been denied a right. There was a time when the American public agreed with the concept of collective bargaining and having a union represent them. This has largely disappeared in the private sector. Unions still do represent some government workers, but they have largely been crippled elsewhere.

The "Right To Work" laws are being put in place supposedly to "protect" workers from being forced to join a union. But I propose in that process, we have done to unions and collective bargaining what any are trying to do to gun ownership – eliminate it.

I have met many people blinded by the argument that collective bargaining and unions forced companies to move their operations overseas. This is an oversimplification of a very complicated issue. A rising tide lifts all boats. What is missing is the rising tide. The right- to- work laws are being adopted to push the working class even farther into commoditization. Without the ability to determine what each of our time is worth and by extension, what condition under which we will work, the employer ends up with an unfair advantage. As we are each commoditized, our value will be determined by someone else. This is a very dangerous place for the American worker.

REASSEMBLING THE INDUSTRIALIZED NATION

With the significant reduction in the size and impact of the organized labor movement in the United States came a move offshore for labor. That came with access to foreign markets as countries negotiated for those commodities (human beings) to use in manufacturing goods to be taxed and manipulated in a global market.

As we look into the United States' labor issue, commoditization was the only way it could go. The cheapening and ultimate disappearance of jobs put all of us in competition with people thousands of miles away. So what was left? Only brain power and left brain skills.

As the pendulum swings back in the other direction, it will take time to assess what part America plays in reassembling the industrial nation we once were. This will require tradesmen and women. It will require vision. And it will require bravery in consideration of the fear that comes from choosing a higher price and lower profit margin in the name of liberty and the long term benefit to an entire nation.

Provided the U. S. remains a Constitutional Republic, re-establishing America as a leader in manufacturing will take time.

A RETURN TO AMERICAN SUPERIORITY

We all need to consider how we return the United States to its place as leader of the free world. In my discussions, many have asked why this is important to us. It is important because our nation depends on its ability to provide the work that is the engine of everything else. Capitalism, free markets and self employment are the breeding ground for innovation, efficiency and the creation of leadership that makes this country great.

Part of the effort to keep our country the leader of the free world will come from establishing, maintaining and defending our place in the industrial and technological world in which we live today. This is a world which no longer views the United States with awe, or respect or even ambition. Rather, much of the world is now engaged in tearing or holding the country down.

As Americans, we once again need a national identity. At one time our "national pride" was a common thread for each of us as we worked to overcome adversity. Through a couple of wars, a few recessions, and many good times, Americans were Americans first, something else second. Now we are a nation of people worried about our own self interests first.

I blame this behavior on politicians and other special interests. I believe the government under the current administration has actually been actively involved in driving American citizens apart at every opportunity.

PROTECTIONISM IS NOT A BAD WORD

When considering the unemployment rate in the U. S. one has only to look at all the jobs being shipped to other countries.

I have watched many conversations where the purchase and sale of commodities originating in other countries has been debated. Certainly, there is a faction that says that we should only buy goods manufactured in this country. When considering this, the term "protectionism" comes up as an argument against that process.

Many individuals will say it is not protectionist, while others tend to discuss why protectionism is not a bad thing. I would like to propose the term protectionism attempts to over-simplify the issue. Let's face it, the methods proposed are protectionism. But protectionism is no more wrong than the protectionism that comes from a foreign country which supplements the export of goods to this country in an effort to run U. S. manufacturers out of business.

BUY AMERICAN

Are we ready to face the concept that buying American produces safety and security for us and our children? I believe Americans are prepared to believe once again that buying American is a national security proposition.

I have watched a number of focus groups and studies that investigated the argument. In many of those discussions, there is a component of people who view what I and others propose as protectionism. The opposition views protectionism as something we should not desire.

I think that may be true from a pure world view, which is where most college and university economics "professionals" are coming from. But I think protectionism in this context is not a bad thing. Certainly, a number of foreign governments have engaged in a process called "dumping", arguably a protectionist approach to their own markets? There have been continuous and ongoing efforts by foreign governments to circumvent U. S. trade policies by whatever means possible. Consider for a moment if a foreign government holds an interest in a car manufacturing company, and that car manufacturing company is losing money on its product, is the foreign government then supplementing the manufacturer, giving it an unfair advantage over another car manufacturer? When considered as a whole, the U. S. has a vested interest in maintaining a "Buy American" attitude in order to ensure the long term security and success of its citizens. Otherwise that foreign automaker, supplemented by a foreign government out to destroy the U. S., will eliminate American domestic manufacturing.

CONSUMERISM AS A WEAPON

It doesn’t take much to be an activist. If you see something wrong, you can simply choose not to participate.

Retail is one of those places where you can make things change simply by where and how you shop.

Consumerism is arguably a good behavior for the American society. Until it begins to propagate behaviors that cause harm to the society as a whole, consumerism will be a key piece of the American Dream.

But at what point does the consumerism begin to do more harm than good? At what point will we each choose that buying that item is not helping the country, and that maybe we can simply do without it?

You can make a difference. When a company openly states their opposition to something you believe in, or when they advocate for something for which you do not care, don’t buy from them any more. Certainly, when they inject themselves into highly contested issues, it is our obligation to correct their perception. As a consumer, your power is greater than you think. Don't hesitate to use your position to get a company's attention as they contribute to the commoditization of you and your future.

THE MINIMUM WAGE DOESN'T MATTER

Many people have been impacted by the federal minimum wage. But try to think of the last time you knew someone who was limited to that amount or whose hourly wage was forced up by the minimum wage.

This is another case of the federal government being a collaborator in deception. The minimum wage has no effect on wages, even for those people who are impacted by it. What the government does to (artificially) increase the bottom end of the scale is simply not enough to make a large difference in a worker's ability to sustain him or herself.

The distinguishing argument is whether government belongs in the business of manipulating the prevailing wage in a free market economy. Certainly, of all the things government does, this one has the least impact. As you have seen throughout this book, the U. S. government, with its many departments, has entered into any number of social engineering projects in the name of their inconsistent agenda on the issues we described.

ELITISM

Are we in danger of becoming, or at least appearing to be, elitists? Absolutely! As we each get comfortable in our own existence, we tend to lose a very important quality of humanity, that of empathy. When we are engaged in life with others, it is quite easy to be an elitist, or to be impacted by someone who has an elitist approach to others.

Look around at how people treat one another and you can tell when their elitism is causing a problem. As a commodity, you will be on the receiving end of this more than you will like. Simply make notes of how that impacts the discussion and move on. Some of those experiences will be challenging as the elitist individual makes very judgmental decisions based on his/her own very limited ability to see beyond the elitist attitude.

It will be valuable to see and learn from this experience. The ability to be a leader and mentor as a manager or consultant can be one of the most satisfying roles as we assist others in surviving in the commoditized world of the future.

POLITICS

There are many areas of the job market and careers that require our ongoing attention - and participation. Be sure to read my book "Return U.S. to Liberty" for a continued discussion on how we can influence our country in the future.

There can be no question that the United States stands at a crossroads today. Regardless of your political leanings, I believe one of the critical occurrences of the last twenty or so years have been the divisive and corrosive infighting between the two "major" national parties. They have simply dragged us into a never ending battle, sometimes having forgotten what battle that was.

Since the 1950's, there has been a move towards less liberty. As we have allowed more government to take control of our lives, we have lost some of the innovative and efficient processes we used to make this country great.

Many in the working class will say they do not have time for politics. They have said that for years. Voter turnout has been quite poor in the last hundred years or so and it shows in the detachment of our representatives.

With all this in mind, it is important that you either remain or get engaged in the political process. It is also important that you work to ensure you are a part of that process, engaging your friends, neighbors, and others in the work that is citizenship in The United States.

Citizen Politician

As you may have begun to realize, this book encourages civil involvement. It should have become quite clear that your involvement in organizations other than work is a central component of your becoming a "well rounded" individual.

As you move through your career, there will be a time when your personal, spiritual and professional lives will intersect. It will be important that you be prepared to embrace that opportunity, especially as a commoditized worker.

GET OUT THE VOTE

It is important to remember that as an American, you are under obligation to vote, to take an active position in holding your representatives accountable to you.

The system of elections in this country has been loaded with inefficiencies, ineffective process and outright fraud.

Most major elections are on a Tuesday. Much of the working class works on Tuesday. This hardly encourages you to take a half day off to vote. But we need to be committed to this obligation and right. What has occurred is many of your jobs have been eliminated as politicians you might not have voted for, or even agreed with, made decisions about your career that were not in your best interest.

POLITICAL PHILOSOPHY

When I went searching for the root cause of the commoditization of America's workforce, it was part of the effort to write a book to help people make the transition to a commoditized career. Nothing surprise me more about this particular book than the emergence of politics as a subject in a book originally conceived to help people define their career and find employment.

What I have concluded is that the American working class got so distracted by their need to maintain a middle class lifestyle that the political machine hijacked their entire existence.

When considering the future, it is important that the United States return to a discussion about the country and how to recover from the devastating blows of the political system corrupted by crony capitalism, bad ethical and moral behavior and all of the issues I mention in the book. What is your personal political philosophy? Have you stopped to consider what is most important to you – and why? Do you allow others to define your opinion, or do you dig in to the issues and fully understand them?

When is the last time you voted, or contacted your Congressman, or met with your Mayor? Over forty percent of Americans have not voted in the last three major elections.[74] [75] Theories abound about why this is the case. From "too much democracy" to a feeling of the vote not having an impact, to the process being inconvenient, lots of us are simply not holding our elected officials accountable.[76]

Political philosophy matters because our employment hinges n the behavior of the United States Government. As you can see in the book, government policy has been the largest factor in the commoditization. Whether it is education, banking, export/imports, unions or any of the other entities mentioned in the book, how these entities behave is influenced by government policy. When we consider the low voter turnout combined with the lobbying efforts of all of those entities, when we don't vote, it is possible those entities discussed in the book are actually determining your future as they go about writing legislation being rubber stamped by the crony capitalists who have bought or are being bought by the

---

[74] http://elections.gmu.edu/voter_turnout.htm

[75] http://en.wikipedia.org/wiki/Voter_turnout_in_the_United_States_presidential_elections

[76] http://www.nbcnews.com/id/49701718/ns/technology_and_science-science/t/why-percent-americans-wont-vote/#.VAmOEst0wdU

political system. You must exercise your rights to control your government in order to ensure you will be able to support your family as the market becomes even more commoditized.

INTEGRITY AND MORALS

Let's start with the textbook definition of integrity: "The quality of being honest and having strong moral principles; moral uprightness."

You know what integrity is, and may have seen more examples of what it isn't than what it is. Almost as important is that you remember that those around you also know what it is. They will be watching for that feature in you. There will be nothing more refreshing than working with someone who knows and appreciates the value of integrity and understands the key impact of collaboration using integrity as a guide.

Unfortunately, the very definition of integrity varies from one social circle to another. Even honesty has been redefined in many circles. Stick with the basics. Treat people with kindness – even when they do not return the favor. Choose to be happy – even when people give you a reason not to be. Set a higher standard – even as the media and others encourage you to engage in a lower standard. Just because you have been commoditized does not mean you need to surrender to a movement to become part of the lower common denominator that is unethical and immoral behavior.

SUMMARY

Technology life cycles, banks, unions, politicians and all of the other entities I mention in this book are fighting for control of the future. Depending on your viewpoint, some of these entities may not have thoughts that align with your idea of how the future should look.

How commoditization impacts your future will depend to some degree on your approach to the future itself. Recognizing commoditization is coming and preparing yourself to be a commodity will help. Developing new methods of supporting yourself and your family will be necessary.

CONCLUSIONS

If we are to reverse the trends of commoditization, the future will need to include the voice of the working class. Whether the future contains a working class and a middle class remains to be seen. There can be no question the trend is downward – a study quoted in the New York Times shows the American Middle Class is no longer the world's richest class.[77]

[77] http://www.nytimes.com/2014/04/23/upshot/the-american-middle-class-is-no-longer-the-worlds-richest.html?_r=0&abt=0002&abg=1

Epilogue

What we see in the commoditized United States is a radically different workforce.

In my career I have learned a significant amount of information. I think we sometimes fail to recognize the influence of others (many successful, and a few not so much). We have the opportunity we have to learn from someone else's courage. Whether they end in success, failure or somewhere in between, so long as we are fully aware of the process and are willing to put energy into the effort to learn, we can benefit from the experience of others.

I am certain this book will help you sort out what it means to have become a commodity. The commoditization of our labor force has been a watershed moment for the country and quite possibly the world. Seeing things through the lens of positive attitude, I am left to believe this new paradigm has occurred for a reason and that the opportunity for success in this innovative time is great.

With this change, I do believe it will become more important that you include responsibility as a citizen in your career plans. The management of your career has never been more important than now as you realize "everything is sales" and that how you researched, applied for, interviewed and obtained a job is a set of tasks not unlike the tending of a garden. As my mother prepared and tended her garden, I was always impressed with the precision and perseverance necessary to make the garden a success. Our

careers require similar attention and planning.
I have worked quite intently on providing you with some help on how to be a commodity. It will take work for some of you to become a commoditized resource. For others it might not be so difficult, but then there will be challenges on a different level.
I believe I have given you insight sufficient to get a new assignment. I believe you also have gained knowledge of the importance of being actively engaged as a citizen of the United States. Finally, I trust you can see what you need to do in order to prepare your skills to make you a marketable commodity......

DEVELOP A SOLID OFFENSE AND DEFENSE

It is important to always be fully engaged in what you believe. Not in what you believe IN, but what you believe!
Develop a solid defense. This requires a dedicated effort to your viewpoint. It is important this is your solid viewpoint, not something you adopted from someone else. There is nothing wrong with advocating a position that is "not normal", provided you can show you have a well thought out defense of that position. I guarantee you will find people who will disagree, but will want you on their team anyway because they know you will give your work that same thought.
Develop a solid offense. Be ready to say what you think and show why this is a good strategy or idea. Someone will question you. Be ready to defend it through solid, offensive strategic thinking. This will require work on your part, requiring a solid approach to tasks

you will encounter and tools you will use in order to have success in your efforts.

LOSE YOURSELF IN SERVICE

One of the first concepts I learned from Anthony Robbins and Stephen R. Covey on my way to changing my life and career was the concept of setting a higher standard.

Find someone to help, and then help them without expectation of personal gain. In other words, "Pay It Forward". There are so many, who feel lost, underappreciated and ignored. But we each bring our own unique skills and talents to the game.

In this mean and hateful world, you will find many who have not gotten a fair shake. Take the opportunity to level the scales, one person at a time. The fulfillment from those experiences cannot be put into words.

In the process, what you will find is that you will fill in all the rough places in your own life. You will find people in much more unfortunate circumstances that will remind you that things can always be worse. You will learn something that you will be useful later in your life. You will make an impact on someone and their family, without compensation. That will leave a lasting mark on your career and your reputation.

PREPARE THE NEXT GENERATION

What do we each owe the next generation? Some will say nothing. Most will not even give the question a thought as to what part they play in passing along their skills and talents to the next generation.

I believe there is a large number of us who have forgotten our individual obligation to prepare the younger generation for their assignment. As I have mentioned, this obligation was filled as unions, employers and individuals went about the business of doing what Americans were uniquely qualified to do; passing on their specialties and skills as they performed the work that made the country great.

"Mentor" is a word not used often enough. The youth of today do not have the advantage of being mentored, appreciated or in many cases, encouraged to reach for new goals. It will become within your power to set the foundation from which the next generation will operate. This will require a great deal of sacrifice and composure on your part as you very deliberately and systematically allow opportunities to pass you by as they get passed on to one of the people you are mentoring. All I can say is "Let it go".

In order for this country to recover, we must have human resources that have been properly prepared for their future, and have been encouraged to develop their natural abilities.

I reiterate that some of my thoughts are not conventional. I trust you will gain new knowledge or a new concept from the book. What is left is for you to decide what to do with that new knowledge. I encourage you to develop a plan for that effort and see it through.

COMMODITIZED

d

From this book, you should be able to see there have been very deliberate efforts to change America, American families, the American way of life and the American Dream.

The way we have been commoditized is as important as the fact that we have been commoditized. It is important to understand all of the causes of commoditization in order to identify how you survive the change.

Who caused this commoditization? I leave you to come to your own conclusions. After reading this book I hope you have a desire to figure it out for yourself.

Why would commoditization be something we want to happen in The United States? The American Dream was a great model. Achieving that dream happened for many in this country. Will commoditization be the destruction of that dream?

As we are being commoditized, how will our lives change and how can we survive? I believe this book will help you begin to plan for your own commoditization.

One thing is certain. You and your future have been commoditized. Recognizing that fact will be the beginning of a better future for us all. Good luck.

About The Author

Wade Burt has been the father to seven children ranging in age from nine to thirty nine years old. He has twelve grandchildren ranging from four to eighteen years old.

Wade has enjoyed a broad background in a variety of roles. His experience with challenges has been extensive and his outlook is reflective of those experiences.

Wade is a healthcare IT consultant, making his living consulting with health care companies on the myriad issues that come from the application of technology to that industry.

Wade is a jack of all trades. His degree is in Avionics. He has been a member of the Ironworkers, Machinists (IAMAW) and other trade unions. He has extensive experience in auto mechanics, home building, home maintenance, aircraft maintenance and a variety of other trades.

At one time, Wade was a Ross Perot Republican, and his political leanings were to the right. In recent years his political approach has moved towards Constitutionalism as he observed the dysfunction that comes from party affiliation. Wade has run for Alderman of a small community and remains involved in politics on a more local level, serving on a number of committees for Congressman Diane Black of Tennessee. Wade acted as a consultant for a U.S. Congress candidate and has formed numerous political websites.

Wade has been involved in community organizations. He served on the Board of the Donelson/Hermitage Rotary Club and was the President of the club for a year.

Wade has produced a number of papers and books on a variety of subjects. He also maintains a website http://www.theworldaccordingtowade.com that presents his thoughts and theories on a wide array of subjects.

Wade's passion is his family. Wade has been divorced from his first wife with whom he had three children. He was married to his wife Teresa, with whom he had another child and a stepson, for 18 years prior to her passing in 2002, after an extended battle with colon cancer. As a widower at age 44, Wade married his current wife Tricia.

Wade lives in Gallatin, Tennessee with Tricia and his two children. His other children live in Texas, Utah, Arkansas and various locations within Tennessee.